Romania

40 Years (1944–1984)

THE WASHINGTON PAPERS

. . . intended to meet the need for an authoritative, yet prompt, public appraisal of the major developments in world affairs.

Series Editors: Walter Laqueur; Amos A. Jordan

Associate Editors: William J. Taylor, Jr.; M. Jon Vondracek

Executive Editor: Jean C. Newsom

Managing Editor: Nancy B. Eddy

MANUSCRIPT SUBMISSION

The Washington Papers and Praeger Publishers welcome inquiries concerning manuscript submissions. Please include with your inquiry a curriculum vita, synopsis, table of contents, and estimated manuscript length. Submissions to *The Washington Papers* should be sent to *The Washington Papers*; The Center for Strategic and International Studies; Georgetown University; 1800 K Street NW; Suite 400; Washington, DC 20006. Book proposals should be sent to Praeger Publishers; 521 Fifth Avenue; New York NY 10175.

Romania

40 Years (1944–1984)

Vlad Georgescu, Editor

Foreword by Eugen Weber

Published with The Center for
Strategic and International Studies,
Georgetown University, Washington, D.C.

PRAEGER SPECIAL STUDIES • PRAEGER SCIENTIFIC

New York • Philadelphia • Eastbourne, UK
Toronto • Hong Kong • Tokyo • Sydney

Library of Congress Cataloging in Publication Data

Main entry under title:

Romania

  (The Washington papers, ISSN 0278-937X ; v. XIII, 115)
  "Published with the Center for Strategic and
International Studies, Georgetown University,
Washington, D.C."
  1. Romania – History – 1944–   I. Georgescu, Vlad.
II. Georgetown University. Center for Strategic
and International Studies. III. Series: Washington
papers ; vol. XIII, 115.
DR267.C56 1985   949.8′03   85-6401

ISBN: 978-0-275-91644-2

Published in 1985 by Praeger Publishers
CBS Educational and Professional Publishing, a Division of CBS Inc.
521 Fifth Avenue, New York, NY 10175 USA

INTERNATIONAL OFFICES

Orders from outside the United States should be sent to the appropriate address listed below. Orders from
areas not listed below should be placed through CBS International Publishing, 383 Madison Ave., New York,
NY 10175 USA

Australia, New Zealand
Holt Saunders, Pty, Ltd., 9 Waltham St., Artarmon, N.S.W. 2064, Sydney, Australia
Canada
Holt, Rinehart & Winston of Canada, 55 Horner Ave., Toronto, Ontario, Canada M8Z 4X6
Europe, the Middle East, & Africa
Holt Saunders, Ltd., 1 St. Anne's Road, Eastbourne, East Sussex, England BN21 3UN
Japan
Holt Saunders, Ltd., Ichibancho Central Building, 22-1 Ichibancho, 3rd Floor, Chiyodaku, Tokyo, Japan
Hong Kong, Southeast Asia
Holt Saunders Asia, Ltd., 10 Fl, Intercontinental Plaza, 94 Granville Road, Tsim Sha Tsui East, Kowloon,
Hong Kong

Manuscript submissions should be sent to the Editorial Director, Praeger Publishers, 521 Fifth Avenue, New
York, NY 10175 USA

Contents

Foreword

U.S. newspaper readers associate Romania with Dracula, the Romanian team's appearance at the 1984 Olympics, and a feisty foreign policy of standing up to the Russians. Such views recall the experience of Dame Edith Sitwell's meeting with Mae West at a London party and remarking that the white dress the actress wore made her look like a Vestal Virgin . . . to which Mae West replied: "Baby, you don't know what you're sayin'!"

The depressing facts in this little book tell us how a naturally wealthy, though underdeveloped, economy has been planned into drab poverty and how a lively society aspiring to democracy has been condemned to a lowest common denominator of misery under the dynastic communism of the Ceauşescu clan. The papers that follow cite chapter and verse to describe an incompetent industry, an agriculture discouraged by collectivization, and a standard of living manipulated to pay for the mistakes of ruling autocrats.

History, says Nicolae Ceauşescu (I paraphrase), does not record consumption, but production. If he is right, history will gloss over mounting food shortages (as the Romanian government does) to note only the failure of industrial policies. The 1964 declaration that "planned [mis]management of the national economy is one of the fundamental . . . attributes of the sovereignty of a socialist state," expresses a basic aspect of the blocked and bureaucratized economy of the East. Economic efficacy is subordinate to political considerations, political debate is limited to the dialectics of pots calling kettles black, and the personality cult relates everything to "the working of a bigoted, though vigorous, mind, greedy of every pretense to hate and persecute those who dissent from his creed." (Gibbon)

By 1982, the Romanian economy was in a state that the *New York Times* described as organized economic disaster. But every cloud has a silver lining: calamity, qualmlessly blamed on the West, facilitated the suppression of dissent. Today, Romania is doing well in paying off its foreign debts on the backs of its people. Sometimes quite literally so. Unable to sell enough of its shoddy, uncompetitive industrial products, it rents out Romanian workmen to labor in the natural gas fields of Central Asia, sells *Volksdeutsche* back to West Germany and, indirectly, Jews to the United States.

Foreign policy, no more successful, also reflects a high degree of irrelevance. Attempts to play the United States or China against the Soviet Union are hampered by geographical realities and, even more, by the fact that Romania is too small a pawn in the great powers' game. And unreliable to boot. Its tendencies to irk the Russians are encouraged from the West and East, but its true nuisance factor is low, especially when compared with the potential of other Soviet satellites.

Communist regimes and those who write about them often refer to Marx as the Inquisition referred to Christ: to explain and justify much that is related to quite different inspirations. Reference to the Soviet Union, also, goes only just so far. One remembers what Amiel wrote in his *Journal Intime* on July 1, 1856: "What terrible masters the Russians would be if they ever should spread the might of their rule over the countries of the South! They would bring us a Polar despotism – tyranny such as the world has never known, silent as darkness, rigid as ice, insensible as bronze, decked with an outer amiability and glittering with the cold brilliance of snow, slavery without compensation or relief; this is what they would bring us."

The Swiss, of course, was right. But the polar despotism that the Russians brought came to Romania following many others. Throughout history, the first priority of too many Romanian shepherds has been to eat their sheep. Nations have the masters, or the parasites, that they accept. Today, in internal as in external affairs, clumsy pretentious autocracy stumbles on, borne by a patient, largely helpless, people long used to exploitation and hard times. Regimes change, the style remains the same.

Eugen Weber
Department of History
University of California, Los Angeles

About the Editor and Authors

Dr. Vlad Georgescu, currently director of the Romanian Service of Radio Free Europe, has taught East European history at several American universities, including Columbia and the University of California at Los Angeles. A Woodrow Wilson fellow from 1979–1980, he has written extensively on Romanian and Balkan history, including *A History of Romania*, published in Romanian by the Romanian-American Academy, Davis, California in 1984.

Serban Orescu is a senior editor with the Romanian Service of Radio Free Europe.

Paul Grafton is an analytical specialist in the Romanian Unit of Radio Free Europe's Research Department.

George Ciorănescu was the chief of the Romanian Unit of Radio Free Europe's Research Department until his recent retirement.

Nestor Ratesh is a senior correspondent in Washington for the Romanian Service of Radio Free Europe.

Simona Schwerthoeffer is an assistant broadcast analyst in the Romanian Section of Radio Free Europe's Analysis Department.

Romania

40 Years (1944–1984)

1

Introduction

Vlad Georgescu

As in most East European countries, communism came to Romania with the Red Army; on the eve of the royal coup of August 23, 1944, in which King Michael joined forces with the Soviet Union to overthrow Marshal Ion Antonescu's pro-German government and bring the country into the Allied camp, the Romanian Communist Party (RCP) had fewer than 1,000 members. Its size, however, did not prove to be a significant factor in its bid for power. Six months after the "liberation" of the country on March 6, 1945, A.I. Vishinsky, Vyacheslav Molotov's deputy, imposed on King Michael, who had been left without any Western support, a government dominated entirely by the Communists. Then, through forgery and intimidation, the party won the elections of November 1946. Although the West protested, the Allied powers signed a peace treaty with Romania in February 1947. From then on, especially after the departure of the Allied Control Commission, the Communist takeover assumed an increasingly rapid and violent pace with the abolition of the National Peasant and National Liberal Parties, the imprisonment of most opposition leaders, the forced abdication of the king, and the proclamation of the People's Republic on December 30, 1947.

Although communism as a system displayed the same

basic characteristics all over Eastern Europe, there were differences from country to country. In Romania, the period beginning December 1947 could be roughly divided into three distinct stages: first Stalinism, covering the 1950s, then the years of limited internal liberalism in the early 1960s and, finally, the successful assertion of Romanian autonomy in 1964. This latter period ended in 1974 with the victory of a new political regime, which is in some respects sui generis. As with many other autonomous socialist regimes, the personality cult is a striking characteristic.

There are practically no elements that distinguished Romanian Stalinism from the original Soviet model: an extremely efficient dictatorship routed practically all opposition, mostly by physical repression. The regime imposed rapid industrialization upon the country, while the peasants were forced into collective farms, which, by 1962, controlled 95 percent of the arable land. The private sector was gradually eliminated, beginning with the banks, the industrial plants, the mines, and then private ownership of homes, restaurants, small shops, medical practices, and taxis. The government implemented two one-year economic plans and then, in 1951, its first five-year plan. Culturally, the regime hoped to create a Romanian *homo sovieticus* by cutting off a Latin-oriented culture from its own roots as well as from its Western sources and by enforcing a policy of Russification. A large number of intellectuals ended up in prison, dead, or removed from public life. By most standards, the 1950s was a period of regression compared to the prewar period of an imperfect, yet perfectible, pattern of modernization.

The leading Communist personality of the period, Gheorghe Gheorghiu-Dej, had been a representative of the "native" Romanian faction of the RCP, with no former Comintern ties and few Moscow contacts. For tactical reasons, Josef Stalin favored him over the "muscovites" and in October 1945 allowed him to become party secretary. Shrewd and ruthless, Gheorghiu-Dej faithfully played the Soviet card, unlike Lucretiu Pătrăşcanu, whose nationalistic statements such as in 1946 — "First I am a Romanian, only then a Communist" —

early on aroused Stalin's suspicions. Allied with the muscovites, Gheorghiu-Dej eliminated Pătrăşcanu first in 1948, then, taking advantage of Stalin's anti-Semitism of later years, eliminated the Ana Pauker, Vasile Luca, and Teohari Georgescu group as well in 1952, becoming the indisputable master of the party.

Nikita Khrushchev's de-Stalinization campaign begun in 1956 was received with great apprehension by RCP leaders in Bucharest, mainly because it was also aimed at replacing the old, discredited East European leaders with reformists. Gheorghiu-Dej vigorously opposed the thesis of the twentieth congress of the Communist Party of the Soviet Union (CPSU) in 1956 by arguing that the Romanians had de-Stalinized already by removing the Pauker faction. The Polish and Hungarian events of October-November 1956 seem to have strengthened Gheorghiu-Dej's position by making the dangers of uncontrolled liberalization so obvious. The Romanian Communists favored the crushing of Imre Nagy's Hungarian government from the very beginning and themselves engaged in a tough repression of students and intellectuals, the two groups most likely to be influenced by the Hungarian and Polish examples. Gheorghiu-Dej's loyalty was rewarded in 1958 by the withdrawal of Soviet troops from Romania. The Soviets apparently thought it useless to continue the occupation of such a faithful ally, especially when a withdrawal might have propaganda gains. They were soon to find out how difficult it is to control even a satellite without military means of intimidation.

During the 1950s a careful observer would have noted the accumulation of potentially conflicting situations between Bucharest and Moscow. The Romanians seem to have asked for the Soviet troop withdrawal as early as 1953, immediately after Stalin's death. Then, in the mid-1950s, the RCP used the concept of national communism for the first time, insisting on a Romanian policy of rapid industrialization, which, although in the best Marxist tradition, was nevertheless opposed by Moscow's more industrialized northern satellites. In 1957, Miron Constantinescu, Central Committee Permanent Bureau member and minister of education, a potential Khrushchevite, was eliminated from the ruling group. A new elite, dominated by technocrats and technocratically inclined apparatchiks, slowly emerged under the leadership of Ion Gheorghe Maurer, Romanian chief of state between 1958 and 1961 and prime minister from 1961 to 1974.

By 1961, Romanian communism had already entered its second stage, characterized by a striving toward external autonomy and internal reform. The new developments were made possible by the changing international situation and the emerging Sino-Soviet split, as well as by the reestablishment of improved Romanian-Western relations. Bucharest began sending economic delegations to Western capitals as early as 1958. It was also in 1958 that the West expressed for the first time its willingness to extend financial credits to Romania, while Romanian trade with the Soviet Union decreased dramatically. Relations with Yugoslavia were also reopened in this period, and, in 1963, Romania's voting pattern in the UN differed from that of the Soviet Union for the first time. Finally, in April 1964, the Romanian Communists opted for neutrality in the Sino-Soviet conflict by publishing their "April Declaration," a document generally considered to be the proclamation of Romania's autonomy.

There are two main ways to explain the Soviet-Romanian split: the first would emphasize the personal conflict between Gheorghiu-Dej and Khrushchev, a conflict generated by the Soviets' desire to impose a new leader in Bucharest as they had in almost all the other East European capitals. The second explanation, without totally rejecting the first one, accents not personalities but policies. The latter explanation emphasizes that, since the late 1950s, the two Communist parties differed sharply over the pattern of modernization to be followed by Romania. Indeed, Khrushchev had revived the Council for Mutual Assistance (CMEA) plan for a socialist division of labor and had encouraged a division between the industrial North and the agrarian South, while Gheorghiu-Dej opposed these plans and insisted on Romania's national right to continue with the classic Marxist concept of industrialization. Thus, the initial conflict was not about the right to be less Marxist and less Communist, but, on the contrary, about Romania's right not to be discriminated against in the process of applying the Marxist economic pattern to Eastern Europe.

The origins of the USSR-Romanian conflict could also be explained by Gheorghiu-Dej's background as a "national Communist" and by the unhappiness of Maurer's technocratic group with the Soviet intention of transforming Romania into an agrarian hinterland of the CMEA. In any case, the results of this split upon the domestic scene were more than encouraging: the last political prisoners were released between 1962 and 1964. The RCP, discovering the political usefulness of nationalism, engaged in a virulent anti-Soviet campaign. Romania's Latin identity was restored, and large portions of the historical past were "rehabilitated." The Russian language disappeared almost overnight from Romanian schools, and the question of the Bessarabian province ceded to the USSR after World War II revived. To the great surprise of many Romanians, the RCP published a strongly anti-Russian collection of Marx's articles, proving Romania's rights to Bessarabia.

Gheorghiu-Dej died unexpectedly in March 1965, at the very beginning of his new course. He was succeeded by a troika—comprised of Nicolae Ceauşescu, first secretary, Stoica Chivu, president of the State Council, Ion Gheorghe Maurer, prime minister—which continued the policies initiated by the former leader. The second half of the 1960s were years of significant diplomatic changes: the establishment of relations with Bonn in 1967, the continuance of good relations with Israel despite the Six Day War, professed sympathy with the Prague Spring experiment, and opposition to the Warsaw Pact invasion of Czechoslovakia in 1968. They were also years of significant domestic progress: the adoption of a new economic system, limiting the importance of central planning and giving more freedom to private enterprise; the encouragement of private initiative, mostly in the consumer sector; the diminution of the role of the individual personnel file that pertained to social origins and former political activities; the encouragement of contact with the West; more freedom for creative artists, writers, and scholars; and an attempt to modernize a "socialist-realist" culture made obsolete by years of Stalinism.

The late 1960s and early 1970s were probably the most prosperous years of the entire postwar period. For the first time since 1944, they were also years of hope. All indications point toward Prime Minister Maurer's technocratic group as the main inspiration behind these trends. The Gheorghiu-Dej supporters seem to have underestimated First Secretary Ceauşescu's political talents, however, and hoped to use him merely as an ally against the old Stalinists, such as Alexandru Draghici, minister of the interior between 1952 and 1965. As party secretary and, since 1967, president of the State Council, Ceauşescu skillfully maneuvered his men into key positions; by the tenth party congress in 1969 he was able to control the Central Committee.

The conflict between Ceauşescu's ideological, apparatchik-oriented mentality and the Maurer technocratic policy became obvious at the beginning of the 1970s. The prime minister was in favor of a balanced and moderate pace of industrialization, without sacrificing the consumer goods' industry, as well as for the continuation of the decentralizing and reformist process. On the other hand, Party Secretary Ceauşescu was pushing toward an even higher rate of accumulation and investment. In the Stalinist tradition, he emphasized huge prestige-bringing projects, mostly in the steel and petrochemical industries.

Ceauşescu apparently believed that fast modernization could be more easily achieved by strict central control and planning. He reversed the initial decentralizing trends and reemphasized the role of political mobilization. After visiting China, Ceauşescu introduced a mini-cultural revolution in July 1971 to weaken the technocrats; the priniciple of cadre rotation was officially adopted in 1972 to make the creation of power bases impossible. His wife, Elena Ceauşescu, became a member of the Political Bureau a year later, and in

1974 Ceaușescu was finally "elected" president of the republic. By then, Prime Minister Maurer had lost all his state and party positions, as had most of the technocrats, who were being replaced by Ceaușescu loyalists.

The eleventh congress of the RCP in 1974 marks the end of the liberal period and the beginning of a presidential regime based on dynastic socialism and a personality cult. Not all Communist societies experienced such a regime; it appeared only in autonomous or independent states such as Albania, North Korea, Romania, China, and the USSR.

Dynastic socialism, at least in the case of Romania, is hardly a metaphor. Through the president's wife, three brothers, a son, and a brother-in-law, to mention only the inner circle, the family directly controls the presidency, the government, such key departments as defense, interior, planning, science and technology, and youth problems – as well as the party cadres. The official propaganda depicts the president as a genius and his wife as a scholar of world renown. Most members of the new elite are authors of many books and great collectors of academic titles and academic awards. They apparently suffer from a deep cultural inferiority complex, usually not typical of dictators. This hagiographic cult reaches amazing heights every January when both the president and his wife, the vice-prime-minister, celebrate their birthdays. As one official journal put it, "He is Romania. We are his sons," and his powers seem to be considered almost supernatural.

Mobilization of support in this manner has no local tradition, the Romanian ruling classes having historically been stronger than the executive and insistent that the princes, kings, or prime ministers not become too powerful. For a developing country such as Romania, this personalization of power certainly has more disadvantages than advantages, the modern gods being in most cases ill-equipped to deal with the complexity of modernization. Their insistence on providing answers for everything usually leads to mistaken strategies and wrong decisions. President Ceaușescu has been led to believe that he knows how to build dams, harvest fields, dig canals, and write history books; specialists are reluctant to do their jobs until they know what the "precious directives" are. The immediate result of this personalization of power has led to serious problems, which seem to deepen each year. Although the international economic slowdown has contributed to Romania's economic stagnation, the main causes for Romania's problems are internal. Instead of introducing incentives, the regime apparently hopes to improve the economic situation by ideological mobilization and administrative measures. Its political strategy looks more like the second serfdom so greatly responsible for the eighteenth century retardation of Eastern Europe than to a strategy of real modernization.

Although much less spectacular than in the 1960s, Romania's foreign policy has maintained its sometimes autonomous course. Unfortunately for the Romanians, this rejection of Moscow's domination is accompanied by an acceptance of Moscow's domestic pattern. The windows to the West are almost closed; most cultural institutions such as the Romanian Academy, the universities, and the research institutes are functioning at a diminished intellectual level. The Romania of the 1980s is dominated by a ruling class that is less developed intellectually and less sophisticated than any former ruling elite.

Most Western observers are struck by the lack of opposition toward such a regime. There are only a few other European countries where the government can regulate by law such aspects of daily life as the temperature of private apartments (15° centigrade), how many kilograms of fruit an individual may consume each year (27), the number of children a woman under 45 years of age is required by law to produce (4), and where the police register private typewriters and any contact with foreigners must be reported to the *Securitate*, Romania's security police.

The Romanian reaction to this regime can be explained in several ways: the first should stress the systematic destruction of most national values, institutions, and individual resistance between 1944 and 1964. Repression was probably more effective in Romania than in any other East European country. External and internal deportation, forced labor on the Danube-Black Sea Canal, and arrests and long prison sentences given many times purely for the sake of intimidation affected at least 1 million Romanians between 1944 and 1964. When internal détente finally did arrive, its nationalistic and anti-Soviet character confused many people, causing them to refrain from open dissent in the hope that once Romanian autonomy was consolidated, the regime would gradually move away from the Soviet domestic pattern. The illusions shattered only at the beginning of the 1970s, when it became clear that independence meant more maneuvering space for the ruling elite, without any real departure from the Soviet model for less favored Romanians. The first organized dissident groups appeared in the more permissive post-Helsinki atmosphere of the late 1970s, only to be crushed one after another. The Romanians were not fortunate enough to have the five minutes of freedom Lenin considered necessary for the takeoff of an opposition movement. Today, only religious dissent is still active, all other forms having been neutralized either by imprisonment or by expulsion of the main dissenters to the West.

For any objective analyst, Communist Romania presents distressing signs of decadence. The economy does not fulfill its basic functions, unable even to feed the population of this former bread basket of Europe. Socialism and forced industrialization have not produced the expected wealth, just poverty. After 40 years of communism, Romania is no longer the promising developing country it once was, but has gradually slipped into a pattern of pseudomodernization.

Are these trends reversible? Socialism's systemic crisis is obviously a phenomenon of long duration, which neither the Romanian Communists nor their allies can solve. but, as some East European countries as well as the late Gheorghiu-Dej and early Ceauşescu years have made quite clear, a certain degree of progress and modernization can be achieved even within the Communist framework, providing the ruling elite is willing to renounce the most extreme and outdated

Marxist clichés and introduce at least parts of the Western economic pattern.

Ceauşcescu, conscious probably of the dangers even a limited economic liberalization could bring to his power monopoly, does not seem inclined to move in this direction, however. The thirteenth party congress held in November 1984 did nothing to change this course. On the contrary, all hopes for a more liberal approach were clearly shattered, the emphasis, as during the past 10 years, being on order, discipline, political and cultural centralism, economic central planning, the increased role of the party and of Marxist ideology, and, obviously, on the cult of the leader. This makes the future of Romania dependent upon a change of the ruling group, an alternative that should not be ruled out completely. After all, not even a Communist ruling elite can afford to accept forever an unsuccessful dictatorship that endangers not only the country's welfare, but its own position as well. Romania may be ripe for a change.

There are few studies on present day Romania; its image has deteriorated steadily. The optimistic forecasts for the country's development of the 1960s have given way to an almost complete lack of interest in Romania in the 1980s. This change is not difficult to understand. Western scholars have shown great sympathy and support for Romania's efforts to increase its autonomy, but any short-lived optimism was shattered when it became clear that the autonomous Romanian Communists proved to be as dogmatic, if not more so, than their former leaders.With a disappointing economy, a foreign policy much less spectacular than it seemed at first, and a disastrous human rights' record, Bucharest has managed to lose most of the creditability it had gained in the West in the 1960s and 1970s.

Our essays do not pretend to cover all the aspects of contemporary Romanian politics. We have only tried to present on the occasion of Romania's fortieth anniversary the main results of the regime that came to power in August 1944. Serban Orescu and Paul Gafton have covered the economy;

George Cioranescu and Nestor Ratesh the foreign policy. Simona Schwerthoeffer analyzes the nationality policy. My own task was to give Romania's four decades of communism a historical perspective. With these brief essays we hope to contribute to the advancement of knowledge about contemporary Romania in the United States.

2

Multilaterally Developed Romania: An Overview

Serban Orescu

The Communist regime in Romania, set up in 1945 under Soviet pressure, adapted its economy to the Soviet model in which the economy was subordinated to the centralized leadership, and priority was given to heavy industry.

The National Conference of the RCP held in October 1945 laid out a broad industrialization plan, which was put into practice after June 1948 when the state nationalized the major means of production. The newly established State Planning Committee then took charge of centralized economic planning. From the beginning, Romania's industrialization policy was autocratic. This accounted for the heavy stress on the exploitation of raw materials and energy resources, quite often regardless of the profitability of the enterprise.[1] A resolution passed by the Central Committee in March 1949 announced the "socialist transformation of the agricultural system," which was to serve as a source of accumulation for rapid industrial development.

Following the Soviet model, Romania concentrated on an extensive development relatively difficult to analyze, partly because of the lack of reliable statistical data.[2] Economic development was characterized by the rapid growth of fixed assets, the movement of workers from the agricultural to the industrial sector, a high rate of accumulation, and a low standard of living. Between 1950 and 1981 the value of fixed assets increased ninefold, which amounted to as much as 2,000 billion *lei* in 1981.[3]

In 1938 the agricultural sector employed 80 percent of the working population.[4] This disproportion was one of the major social problems in prewar Romania. By 1981, the percentage had dropped to 28.6.[5] The per capita national income grew from $100 in 1938, to $2540 in 1981.[6] The percentage of accumulated national income rose from 17.6 percent in 1951–1955 to 36.3 percent in 1976–1980.[7] In 1983 the rate of accumulation dropped to 31 percent as a result of the worldwide economic crisis.[8]

The same crisis caused a reduction in the volume of investment, as compared to 1979, after a long period of steady growth. Between 1965 and 1980 about 50 percent of the total volume of investment was allocated to industry. The impressive growth of investment in the machine-building sector – from 7 percent of the total volume allocated to industry in 1965 to 28 percent in 1980, dropping to 21 percent in 1981 – provides another indication of the autocratic character of Romania's economic policy, even in a period of recession.[9]

The size of the industrial enterprises is typical of Romania's large-scale economy. In 1960 the average number of employees for each enterprise was 747, but the figure rose to 1,830 by 1982. As a result of this process of concentration, local industries were, practically speaking, amalgamated into a national industry. The number of enterprises subordinated to local People's Councils dropped from 318 in 1950 to only 22 in 1982, while the number of employees decreased from 149 thousand to 25 thousand.[10]

The regime managed to create a relatively balanced equilibrium in the economic structure of the country by emphasizing the distribution of industrial investment to mainly agricultural regions, which might explain the rather peculiar location of an iron and steel plant at Calarasi, in the richest grain-farming zone of the Baragan. This made rapid industrial employment of the rural population possible, but it also explains why the professional qualifications of the new employees were rather low.

Between 1965 and 1980, investment policies generally gave preference to advanced technological equipment, largely imported from the West. The emphasis was on extensive investments in modern equipment, not on a more efficient use of capital assets. But the tendency to save on training costs and spare parts and reduce maintenance personnel led to stoppages and losses of working time.

Nonetheless, according to official statistics, industrial production was 34 times larger in 1982 than in 1938, which means a growth rate of almost 12 percent per year. The portion of the national income originating in industry grew from 30.8 percent in 1938 to 55.7 percent in 1982.[11] The numbers of employed grew as well. Compared to about 1 million employed in 1950, the industrial enterprises were employing about 3.3 million in 1982. Labor productivity in the industrial sector was also 9.6 times higher than in 1950; this equals an annual growth rate of 7.3 percent.[12]

Industrial development was not based on thorough economic and technological studies, however. The major targets were set by the Central Committee, while the ministries and enterprises strove to confirm established targets, often by manipulating the efficiency indicators. Performance was largely judged on the basis of achieving volumetric targets, instead of improving efficiency, and the Central Committee was presented with new programs that exist only in theory. Under these conditions some of the industrial capacities exceeded market requirements.

Rather than encouraging the research sector, the government lowered the reward ceiling for inventions and innovations in 1974 to three months' salary. As a result, patent applications sank from 4,500 in 1976 to 3,300 in 1980.[13] For similar reasons obsolete machinery was retained or parts of it were reused, although they were worn out. In February 1982, President Ceauşcescu recommended that scrap automobile bodies be recycled and used for new automobiles.[14] The result of such a policy was a loss in quality and a decrease in labor productivity.

Because Romanian industry did not generate enough currency through its exports to import goods upon which the industry depended, exports of agricultural goods had to provide an important part of the necessary currency. This of course affected the standard of living and the balance of payments.

The failure of this strategy of extensive development became more evident when the flood of peasants from rural areas into industrial regions decreased. Rapid industrial expansion had to be supported more and more by technical progress and the growth of labor productivity, as well as improvements in efficiency and marketability — factors that the Romanian economy has been unable to master. At present, more than half the fixed assets are not more than 10 years old, but the results are still not satisfactory.

The agricultural sector reflects the same pattern of quantitative rather than qualitative development. Despite its importance for the economy, Romanian agriculture remains significantly below its potential. Undoubtedly raising yields by better controlling and timing of field operations is possible. Although Romania is far from being an important exporter of agricultural products, an increasing share of total agricultural produce has been exported. This was accomplished by diverting goods from the domestic market, illustrating the failure of the regime to stimulate intensive agricultural growth. There are 2.25 acres of arable land per capita. Slightly more than three-quarters of an acre (0.85) would be sufficient to assure a nutritional basis for the population should the government decide to shift to a policy of intensive farming.

In February 1981, at the second congress of the agricultural councils, President Ceauşescu pointed out that the overwhelming emphasis laid on industrial development did in fact result in overlooking the importance of agricultural production. He called for a totally new agricultural policy to raise production and labor productivity.[15] After crop yields of 19.9 million tons in 1981 and 22.3 million tons in 1982, yields fell to about 20 million tons in 1983, although more than one-quarter of all arable land was irrigated.[16] To raise grain yields, 60 percent of the arable regions were planted with cereals. To attain larger yields, the rotation of wheat and maize was practiced, although this leads to a reduction in soil fertility.[17] As part of the same policy of extensive development, plans have been made to expand the irrigated area to 27.5 million acres by 1989 (in contrast to 11.5 million at the end of 1982).[18] This implies high investments, which, according to official data, would be raised to 100 billion *lei*.[19] Unfortunately, fertilizers are not sufficiently applied (34–36 kilograms [kg] per acre), although great quantities were exported, totaling about 2.7 million tons in 1982.[20] The situation is no better with manures. Instead of increasing the application of fertilizers, Romania preferred to import maize from South Africa in 1982 in exchange for 200 thousand tons of fertilizers.[21]

Some experts believe that the low productivity of Romanian agriculture is a result of the lack of financial stimulation offered to peasants, both in the socialized and in the private sectors. The delivery of agricultural products is considered a sign of the worker-peasant alliance. This old ideological concept has priority over material incentives. Thus, although on the average 20 peasants are employed for every 500 acres (which is more than enough), crop losses have risen to between 30 and 45 percent.[22]

Ceauşescu was right when he said in 1979 that production could be doubled.[23] But the way agriculture is managed in Romania makes the successful implementation of such a plan unlikely.

The Economic Mechanism

At the beginning of the 1960s the East European countries followed the Soviet example and announced a new decentralized pattern of economic development. Romania, in 1967, was the last socialist country to join this plan of reform. This delay may have been the result of conflicting views in the RCP regarding decentralization of authority. Ceauşescu's wing of the party opposed decentralization, while some technocrats, led by Prime Minister Maurer, were in favor of it.

After the National Conference of the Communist Party in 1967, the government published the new directives for more efficient economic management and planning. Nevertheless, the reduction of plan indicators provided by these directives was not reached, and, in the 1970s, the number of indicators started to increase again.

The founding of new, centralized industrial organs, which took over some of the functions of the industrial enterprises, only meant a new form of centralization in the decision-making process. In the mid-1970s a new concept was elaborated: the "unique national plan," which was to involve the human and material resources of the entire nation. This plan reflected Ceauşescu's desire to further enhance the role of the party. Ceauşescu's demand that the central plan should include a complete list of the entire production reflects the strongly centralized character of Romanian economy.[24]

The economic crisis that started in 1975 forced the regime to adopt a new strategy. At the beginning of 1978, President Ceauşescu announced reforms meant to "destroy the old mechanisms and to replace them with new ones."[25] This was not a step toward the Yugoslav economic model, however. By self-management and self-administration the regime did not call for more autonomy in decision making, but rather the Soviet notion of *hozrasciot* — a "thrifty household" — meaning a household not financed by the state.

The principal plan indicator within this new mechanism became "net production." The use of net production as a success indicator, according to which wages are recalculated, met with difficulties. By September 1983, the emphasis laid on this indicator had diminished, and net production was given the same status as material production and sales.[26] Because personal income depended on such a great number of indicators, workers' discontent grew.

The Standard of Living

The data related to the reduction of the standard of living in Romania in the past years is inconsistent. (The standard of living is defined as the total value of consumption goods and services provided to one person.) According to confidential information given by the Romanian government to the International Monetary Fund (IMF) in 1983, Romania's standard of living has decreased in recent years by 19 percent. In the opinion of the IMF, the actual figure is 40 percent.[27] In August 1978, President Ceauşescu admitted that "on the whole, socialist countries are not succeeding in providing consumption goods according to needs, and in particular, they have not kept pace with the demand for food products."[28]

Between 1950 and 1972 the standard of living apparently increased slowly but steadily. Its decrease started slowly at first and became more rapid after 1978. The decrease registered in recent years is a result of Romania's efforts to reduce the amount of consumer goods on the internal market, done partly at the suggestion of the IMF to increase exports and improve the balance of trade.[29] Western experts estimate that in 1983 the price of consumption goods rose by about 6 percent, which meant a decrease in actual consumption by about 13 percent.[30] The highest rise in prices took place in 1982, when the inflation rate for 220 consumer goods rose to 35 percent.[31] In June 1982, electricity costs increased by 30 percent, and natural gas by 150 percent. In October 1981, bread, wheat, and maize and grain products were rationed to provide only 150 kg of wheat and 30 kg of maize per year.[32] In practice, rationing included other food products such as eggs, oil, butter, meat, and sugar. This was a return to the ration card system practiced in the early 1950s. Starting in October 1981, people who were found with food exceeding the basic needs of a family could be accused of blackmarketeering and punished with five years in prison. In an effort to influence public opinion, the government started propaganda compaigns against exaggerated consumption of meat and sugar. Western reports and even those in other socialist countries have constantly mentioned the shortage of food in Romania. According to official data, the per capita consumption of meat and fish rose to 68 kg in 1982, but outside experts consider that the consumption was substantially lower.[33] The food scarcity led to symptoms of malnutrition because of lack of animal proteins, a situation even worse in rural areas,[34] and in July 1982, the government published a "scientific nutrition program," which determined basic needs according to the energy lost in the working process.[35] But the standard of living is certainly not a main concern of the regime. Ceaușescu said in 1980 that "history did not record the amount of consumption goods as it did the efforts undertaken to develop productive forces and to secure the future of the nation."[36]

A law introduced in October 1982 obliged employees eventually to buy "social shares" of their enterprises so that they would have a greater interest in the success of their factories.[37] In 1983, minimum guaranteed wages were abolished, and a 10.4 percent general increase in the nominal wage was announced.[38] Pay now depends on how well the worker performs and how well his factory measures up to production targets. This, however, would not cover the increase in the cost of living by any means. The apparent growth of real personal income proved to be even more of an illusion when it is taken into consideration that the weight of the variable part of wages (the part that depends on the accomplishment of production targets) has increased, while the fixed part is decreasing. In the countryside a barter economy has developed, in which some goods can be bought only in exchange for agricultural products, replacing the monetary exchange system.[39]

Industrialization

Romania's rapid industrialization, with special emphasis on heavy industry, was meant to achieve both political and economic goals. The economic goal was the modernization of a predominantly agrarian economy. The political goal was the changing of social, economic, and political relations between classes and individuals within the society. By increasing the effective strength of the working class, the regime considered itself more legitimate.[40] The growth and increasing importance of heavy industry within the national economy also generated an increased demand for resources that was detrimental to other branches such as agriculture, light industry, and the food industry. It is worthwhile to examine some of the specific industries whose importance has been stressed by the regime in Bucharest: the energy, the iron and steel, the machine-building, and the chemical industries.

Energy

Energy plans in Romania call for 90 percent of its power consumption to be covered by domestic resources by 1985. According to this plan, Romania is to become totally energy self-sufficient in 1990.[41] Within this program of "economic independence," a major emphasis has been placed on the domestic petroleum and coal industries.

Oil output has grown from 6.6 million tons in 1938 to 11.6 million tons in 1983, peaking in 1975 at 14.6 million tons. According to its plans, Romania should produce 13 million tons in 1984 – an amount many experts consider unrealistic. Large investments have been allocated to oil drilling on the continental platform of the Black Sea – with no results as yet – and all drilling depth is to increase to 8-10 thousand meters from 6.5 thousand in an attempt to counteract declining oil production.[42] Especially after 1979, however, long-term profitability and the possible exhaustion of the domestic resources were not taken into account. According to some U.S. evaluations, should oil production continue at its present rate, Romanian oil resources will be exhausted by the beginning of the 1990s. The natural gas output has grown faster than the oil output, from 311 million cubic meters in 1938 to 32,600 million in 1983.[43] But Romanian experts say that these resources will be exhausted by the year 2010.[44] According to the "directive" of the thirteenth party congress of the RCP, the extraction of oil and natural gas should decline considerably in 1986-1990.[45]

Net coal production rose from 2,208 million tons in 1938 to 44,500 million tons in 1983; lignite production increased

127-fold between 1938 and 1982, but pit coal and anthracite output increased only 4.1-fold.[46] The plan for the coal industry projects net coal production at 87 million tons in 1985, which, again, seems unrealistic.[47]

The construction of nuclear power stations was announced in 1965 at the ninth congress of the RCP. At that time nuclear power was considered the best option for a country with limited natural resources. The commissioning date for any nuclear power station, however, has been successively postponed. The latest postponement sets back the possibility of any construction until at least 1990.

Romania set ambitious targets for its electricity section, but 1981–1983 was marked by serious problems. At the end of 1983, the population was asked to reduce energy consumption by 50 percent. This came after a previous reduction of 20 percent in June 1982. These reductions came in spite of increases in electric output, according to official statistics.

Electric power output increased from 1,130 million kilowatts (kw) in 1938 to 68,900 million kw in 1982.[48] At the same time, the capacity of the electric power stations grew from 501 thousand kw in 1938 to 17.4 million kw in 1982.[49] By capitalizing on the hydroelectric potential of the Danube and other major rivers, the hydroelectric output rose at a spectacular pace from 148 million kw in 1938 to 11.8 million kw in 1981. In 1982 the hydroelectric output rose to 17 percent of the total energy production, an 80-fold increase from 1938. Within the same period of time thermoelectric energy output increased 58-fold.[50] The share of Romania's electric power produced by gas, oil, or crude oil rose from 5.5 percent in 1965 to 12.9 percent in 1980, even though the country had to import petroleum and other fuels and despite the international oil crisis.[51]

Romania's main reaction to the international crisis was to use inferior coal in thermoelectric plants, a program that called for the opening of a power station based on bituminous shales in Anina. Some experts have raised doubts about Romanian policy in this field. They point out that the total investment is about 2.5 times higher in plants working on the basis of coal and bituminous shales, and the inferior quality of the lignite has a negative influence on the efficiency of power units.

Iron and Steel

The development of the iron and steel industry was a major concern to the RCP as early as 1945. Romania's steel production rose from 284,000 tons in 1938 to 12.6 million tons in 1983. To a certain extent against the wishes of its CMEA partners, Romania started to construct an integrated iron and steel plant in Galati in 1964. This involved three steel works equipped with oxygen converters, which were to have a final output of 10 million tons of steel. In the mid-1970s the construction of a similar plant was started in Calarasi.

According to directives of the eleventh congress of the RCP in 1974, these huge investments in iron and steel were meant to ensure the production of 25–27 million tons of steel by 1990.[52] The directives of the thirteenth party congress reduced this target to 20 million tons.[53] The implementation of these plans seems doubtful, however, considering Romania's financial and energy resource situation.

The iron ore situation is of particular concern. Romanian iron ores are of limited utility and involve high processing costs.[54] Iron ore extraction increased from 139 thousand tons in 1938 to 2.1 million tons in 1982, but this amount still falls far short of covering the needs of the iron and steel industry, where there are thought to be about 20 million tons per year. The expansion of ore extraction would entail increased specific investments and production costs. In any case, experts consider that at the present rate of extraction, iron ore resources will be exhausted by 1990.[55]

Machine-Building

The Communist regime expanded the existing machine-building plants in June 1948, at the time they were nationalized. This was followed by the construction of a great number of new plants, initially supplied with Soviet and East German equipment and, after 1964, replaced by Western equipment and technology. Especially since 1980, however, there has been a tendency to produce everything domestically if technically possible. The expansion of the industry has led to an increased output 202 times greater in 1982 than in 1938.[56] Romania was in tenth place in the world in machine tool production in 1983.[57]

The tendency toward large-scale enterprises with a low level of specialization led to the construction of huge enterprises in this sector. Each enterprise in the machine-building sector now has an average of 3,000 employees. The quality of the goods produced is below international standards, except for a few products like oil equipment, in which Romanian industry has achieved remarkable results.

Chemicals

Another important industrial branch is the chemical industry. Its output multiplied 321 times between 1938 and 1982.[58] Oil and natural gas, salt and nonferrous ores, and sulphur deposits are the main raw materials of the Romanian chemical industry.

The petrochemical branch of the industry has been developed with no concern for the worldwide recession that began in 1974 when oil prices rose at a higher rate than processed products. Despite the fact that limited domestic oil resources necessitated the import of 12.9 million tons of oil in 1981, paid for in hard currency, the volume of investment in petrochemistry grew even during the oil crisis years, and a new petrochemical plant was constructed in Navodari near Constanta in 1977. As a result, only 50 percent of the processing capacity of the petrochemical industry (approximately 34 million tons) was utilized in 1984. Moreover, the petrochemical industry, being a large consumer of hard currency, contributed to Romania's currency scarcity of 1981 that led to the decrease in the total volume of oil imports. Thus, it is indirectly a major cause of Romania's current economic crisis.

Foreign Trade

Since 1971, Romania has been a member of the General Agreement on Tariffs and Trade (GATT). The United States first granted Romania the most favored nation status in 1975. At the same time, the European Community established a preferential tariff status for Romania.

Between 1950 and 1982 foreign trade grew by a factor of 34.[59] In 1983 the volume of foreign trade (303.7 billion *lei*) was, however, 8.6 percent lower than in 1981 and 19 percent lower than planned.[60] The per capita export volume is relatively low – $370 in 1978, as compared to $594 in Hungary and $849 in Bulgaria.[61]

During the first decade after the war, Romania's foreign trade was oriented toward the Soviet Union and other Eastern countries. It was not until a meeting of the RCP Central Committee in November 1958 that the first steps toward an increase in trade with Western countries were taken.[62] This shift reflected Romania's new industrialization plans opposed, by its CMEA partners. This approach toward international economic relations has been intensified since President Ceauşescu came to power, although it has not improved the marketability of Romanian exports within the developed market economies.

The increase in trade with nonsocialist countries was accompanied by a parallel reduction in trade with those of the CMEA – from 66.6 percent in 1960 to only 31.5 percent in 1980. The volume of trade with the Soviet Union decreased even more spectacularly, from 40 percent in 1960 to 18 percent in 1981.[63] After 1980, however, because of lack of hard currency and an increasing indebtedness to the West, Romania tried to increase its trade volume with CMEA countries again, especially to fulfill its crude oil and other raw material needs.[64]

After 1970 Romania intensified its trade with developing countries, increasing it from 8.2 percent in 1970 to 27 percent in 1981.[65] With that end in view it secured loans to these countries totaling $3 billion between 1960 and 1980.[66] The growth of the trade volume with the developing countries is based on oil imports, as well as exports of armaments (mainly to Egypt), and complex technical equipment.[67]

During the past years, Romania has reduced its imports from developed market economies in order to balance its payments in convertible currency. Import cuts implemented after 1981 were followed by a decrease in export capacity, resulting in a lowering of the total volume of foreign trade. In 1982 trade volume with West Germany decreased by 40 percent, with France by 30 percent, and with the United States by 50 percent.[68] On the whole, exports to nonsocialist countries were reduced by 15.6 percent and imports by 33.3 percent, ensuring Romania of an important surplus.[69]

The country still faces a dilemma: either to reduce the imports further, which would lead to a waste of processing capacities, or to face a chronic deficit in its balance of payments. This deficit rose to 3.8 billion *lei valuta* in 1978, 5.3 billion in 1979, and 8.0 billion in 1980.[70] After 1980, a drastic reduction of imports and the forced export of food products (which, obviously, affected the standard of living) resulted in a surplus in the commercial balance; 3.0 billion *lei* in 1981, and 26.9 billion *lei* in 1982.[71] The further reduction of imports remains a constant goal. President Ceauşescu pointed out that a condition for the implementation of the annual plan for 1985 would be to keep the total value of imports below $2.2 billion, a proposal that is probably unrealistic.[72]

Romania's exports are partly based on dumping prices.[73] Cooperation in the industrial sector plays an important part in its foreign trade policy, which provides Romania with technical assistance and allows joint projects with developed countries.[74] One form of production-oriented joint ventures has involved foreign capital. But out of the seven industrial concerns of this type founded in Romania after 1971, only four are still functioning.[75]

Romania's foreign debt increased rapidly in the 1970s as a result of its economic policy coupled with the worldwide increase in oil prices and the interest on loans. In the summer of 1981, Romania began to have repayment difficulties.

Its foreign debt rose from $1.1 billion in 1971 to $10.1 billion in 1981, decreasing in 1983 to $9.0 billion.[76] The net debt in convertible currency on December 31, 1982 could be listed as follows:[77]

• debts to commercial banks	$5,421.1 million
• debts to contractors with bank guarantees	307.4
• credits from international financial institutions:	
International Monetary Fund	930.9
World Bank	1,485.5
Bank for International Settlements in Basel	100.0
• debts for imports of goods and services	1,108.0
• credits from socialist international banks	413.3
Total:	$9,766.2

A major part of Romanian foreign debts had to be repaid between 1981 and 1983; this and higher international interest rates forced Romania to ask for a new rescheduling of payments up to 1989.[78] In June 1981, as a member of the IMF since 1972, Romania obtained a standby credit of about $1.5 billion to improve its financial situation.[79]

In February 1984 Romania cancelled the last ($285 million) tranche of its standby credit due from the IMF, apparently because its external finances had improved while IMF policy conditions had become increasingly irksome. According to some experts, Western loans enabled Romania to avoid economic reforms that would have raised the competitive quality of its products. At present, the regime's efforts are concentrated on preserving Romania's economic system as it is. Another goal is to increase the surplus of the commercial balance of payments, mainly by lowering the standard of living, to avoid any further rescheduling of its foreign debts.

Conclusions

The Romanian economic crisis has several causes. First, there is the failure of Romania's socialist model, which, in turn, is a part of the overall failure of the socialist model as a whole. By overexaggerating some characteristics of the socialist model, Ceauşescu's socialism aggravated the country's situation. Second, as its economy was exposed to the fluctuations of the international economy by its intermingling with capitalist economies, Romania's economic crisis is also a result of the worldwide recession.

By adhering to certain ideological clichés and subordinating economic efficiency to political considerations, the Romanian state and party leaders demonstrate that they do not fully understand economic laws nor the mechanism of socialist economies. President Ceauşescu's regime continues to aggravate the crisis by laying a strong emphasis on mobilization and political activism, by rejecting any form of decentralization, by promoting people to management positions according to their political loyalties, and last, by encouraging a hostile policy toward intellectuals, whom he considers a threat to his regime.

Ceauşescu apparently believes the best way to improve his country's economic situation is with more, not less, communism; as he declared at the November 1984 thirteenth party congress, "We have to bear in mind that we cannot weaken . . . the centralized management of the social economic activity based on the central plan." Under such a policy, the current economic crisis has every chance of worsening.

Notes

1. According to the 1974 party program the investment and production targets are not related to the capitalist criterion of maximum profit but to the socialist principle of developing productive forces. See *Scînteia*, September 1, 1974: "the party put industrialization in the center of the socialist organization of the economy, in particular the development of heavy industry. . . . "

As Nicolae Ceauşescu put it: "The leading sector in the socialist economy is industry, with a strong emphasis given to heavy industry," *Scînteia*, June 2, 1966.

2. There are reasons to believe that the government also uses statistical data as an instrument of propaganda. Official statistics often operate with units of measure that cannot be compared. Because an accurate comparison of the data is not possible, all these figures should therefore be read with care. Alteration of data takes place at the ministerial or even lower levels, prompted by the desire to present the government in the best possible light. See M. R. Jackson, *Assessments of Economic Information from Bulgaria and Romania* (Tempe, Ariz.: Arizona State University, no year of publication); *Romania, The Industrialization of an Agrarian Economy* (Washington, D.C., 1979), 81.

3. *Anuarul Statistic al R.S.R., 1983* (Statistical Yearbook of the Socialist Republic of Romania, 1983) (Bucharest: Directia Centrala de Statistica, 1983), 44.

4. N. Spulber, *The Economics of Communist Eastern Europe* (New York: John Wiley & Sons, 1957), 5. In other East European countries the percentages were as follows: Yugoslavia, 76.3 percent; Hungary, 51 percent; Poland, 65 percent; Czechoslovakia 25.5 percent.

5. *Anuarul Statistic al R.S.R., 1983*, p. 58.

6. The per capita national income is a value-added concept measured in delivery prices and the sum of net products in the productive sector, in which net product equals global product less material expenditure. (It does not include the net products of the nonproductive sector or depreciation expenditures.) For statistical data see N. Spulber, "Changes in the Economic Structures" in Charles and Barbara Jelavich, eds., *The Balkans in Transition* (Hamden, Conn.: Archon, 1974), 359 and *World Bank Annual Report 1983* (Washington, D.C.: World Bank, 1983).

7. *Anuarul Statistic al R.S.R., 1982*, p. 49.

8. *Scînteia*, November 20, 1984.

9. *Anuarul Statistic al R.S.R., 1983*, p. 202.

10. *Anuarul Statistic al R.S.R., 1983*, p. 70.

11. Ibid., 44, 45.

12. Ibid., 42, 58.

13. N. N. Constantinescu, "Posibilităti incomplet folosite pentru promovarea intensă a progresului tehnic" (Unused Means of Increasing Technical Progress) in *Era Socialistă*, no. 5 (1982), 13.

14. *Scînteia*, December 9, 1982.

15. Ibid., February 20, 1981.

16. Ibid., December 10, 1983.

17. *Anuarul Statistic al R.S.R., 1983*, 137; "Concepţia partidului nostru, a tovarăsului Nicholae Ceauşescu, despre locul şi rolul agriculturii in economia naţionala" (The Concept of the Party and of Nicolae Ceauşescu Concerning the Place and Role of Agriculture within the National Economy) in *Era Socialistă*, no. 7 (1983), 31; see also *Scînteia*, April 23, 1983.

18. *România liberă*, July 2, 1983.

19. *Scînteia*, July 1, 1983: According to some specialists the costs needed to improve the soil quality would rise to ca. 600 billion *lei*; see also D. Teaci, "Agricultura, componenta a creşterii economice" (Agriculture, Part of Economic Development) in *Revista Economica*, no. 52 (1981), 9.

20. *Anuarul Statistic al R.S.R., 1983*, 259.

21. *Frankfurter Allgemeine Zeitung*, February 13, 1982.

22. "Oprea Parpală, Autoconducerea teritorială" (Territorial Selfdetermination) in *Tribuna*, no. 51 (1982).

23. *Scînteia*, March 8, 1979.

24. Ibid., May 15, 1976; Iosif Dumitru Bati, "Probleme ale echilibrului în procesul creşterii economice" (Problems of Equilibrium in the Process of Economic Growth) in *Era Socialistă*, no. 17 (1981), 5.

25. *Scînteia*, February, 18, 1978.

26. *Buletinul Oficial I*, no. 70 (1983).

27. *Frankfurter Allgemeine Zeitung*, February 17, 1983. The Statistical Yearbook (*Anuarul Statistical R.S.R.*) does not include data on variations in the standard of living.

28. *Scînteia*, August 4, 1983.

29. Reuters, June 11, 1983.

30. *Review of the Second Romanian Economic Memorandum to Western Banks, Part I* (Philadelphia, Penn.: Wharton Econometric Forecasting Associates, March, 22, 29, 1983), 3. See also *Anuarul Statistical R.S.R., 1983*, p. 243. According to official data, the price increase for these products between 1970 and 1981 was only 12.1 percent – a similarly unrealistic figure.

31. Radio Free Europe Research(RFER), *Romanian Situation Report*, no. 4 (1982).

32. *România Libera*, June 30, 1982; RFER, *Background Report*, no. 149 (July 16, 1982) (Romania); *Scînteia*, October 18, 1981.

33. *New York Times*, December 27, 1983; *Christian Science Monitor*, January 10, 1984. *Scînteia*, December 29, 1982.

34. Siebenbürgische Zeitung, September 15, 1984, p. 2.

35. Ibid., July 14, 1982. The program that mentioned an average per capita consumption of 68–70 kg meat and fish, 210–230 liters of milk and milk products, 260–280 eggs, etc., turned out to remain valid only in theory. The supply program for 1983–1984 contains per capita consumptions 25–30 percent lower, which, as a matter of fact, are also unattainable. *Scînteia*, December 17, 1983.

36. *Scînteia*, December 24, 1980.

37. *România Liberă*, October 12, 1983.

38. *Buletinul Oficial I*, no. 69 (September 13, 1983) and no. 70 (September 17, 1983).

39. *România Liberă*, July 2, 1983.

40. " . . . the working class being closely related to the most advanced form of material production – heavy industry – it follows that at the same time, it is the most consequent revolutionary class," editorial in *Scînteia*, December 13, 1977.

41. See Ceauşescu's speech at the national conference of the party in *Scînteia*, December 17, 1982.

42. At the twelfth congress of the RCP in November 1979, Nicolae Ceauşescu announced that oil extraction in the Black Sea would start in the near future.

43. *Scînteia*, January 29, 1984.

44. Călin Mihăileanu and Mario Duma, "Implicaţii ştiinţifice, economice şi sociale ale asigurării independenţei energetice a ţării" (Scientific, Economic, and Social Implications of the Energy Self sufficiency) in *Era Socialistă*, no. 16 (1982), 17–19.

45. *Scînteia*, September 5, 1984.

46. *Anuarul Statistic al R.S.R., 1983*, 90.

47. *România Liberă*, April 2, 1982.

48. *Scînteia*, March 9, 1982; *Anuarul Statistic al R.S.R., 1983*, 90.

49. *Anuarul Statistic al R.S.R., 1983*, 96.

50. Ibid.

51. Ibid., 97.

52. *Scînteia*, August 3, 1974.

53. Ibid., September 5, 1984.

54. Florian Neagu, "Cerinţa unor schimbări de fond în cercetarea tehnico-ştiinţifică miniera" (The Need for Basic Changes

in Technical and Scientific Mining Research) in *Era Socialistă*, no. 6 (1982), 5–8.

55. Ibid.

56. *Anuarul Statistic al R.S.R., 1983*, 76.

57. "Machine Tools Post a Slow Year" in *American Machinist* (February 1984), 76.

58. *Anuarul Statistic al R.S.R., 1983*, 76.

59. Ibid., 42. An evaluation of Romanian foreign trade after 1980 compared to its previous performance is rather difficult because of the change in reference indicators (*lei* instead of *lei valuta*). One *lei valuta* equals about 3.3 *lei*.

60. *România Liberă*, February 28, 1981, December 10, 1982; *Scînteia*, January 29, 1984.

61. Data refer to 1978. See *Statistic Yearbook of ONU, 1979, 1980*, pp. 496–499. In 1964 Romanian per capita exports amounted to $53 per inhabitant. See John Michael Montias, *Economic Development in Communist Romania* (Cambridge, Mass.: MIT Press, 1967), 147. See also Ioan Georgescu, "Relaţiile economice internaţionale ale României" (Romania's International Economic Relations) in *Revista Economică*, no. 28 (1983), 15.

62. Montias, *Economic Development*, 201.

63. D. Ghermani, "Rumänien und der RGW" (Romania and the Comecon) in *Südosteuropa*, no. 9 (1983), 503.

64. The oil imports from the Soviet Union decreased by 91 percent in 1982 compared to 1981. See *Review of the Second Romanian Memorandum to Western Banks, Part III*, no. 24. (Philadelphia, Penn.: Wharton Econometric Forecasting Associates, April 4, 1983), 2.

65. Ovidiu Rujan, "România, participantă activă la diviziunea internaţională a muncii" (Romania Active Participant in International Labor Division) in *Revista Economică*, no. 52 (1982), 11.

66. See "Romanian Credits to Other Countries," RFER, *Background Report* no. 180 (December 22, 1975). Romania is among the leading East European countries (other than the Soviet Union) that grant credits to developing countries. See *Die Welt*, April 5, 1978.

67. *New York Times*, September 29, 1983.

68. *Frankfurter Allgemeine Zeitung*, February 10, 1983; *Le Monde*, April 21, 1983; RFE/Radio Liberty (RL), CN 115, (April 18, 1983) (CND/Special).

69. Wharton, *Review, Part III*, p. 1. In August 1981, Nicolae

Ceauşescu said: "We covered the needs of the population by completely renouncing exports." See *Scînteia*, August 30, 1981. On the other hand, on July 5, 1978, he said that "agriculture has also to cover the costs of imports of raw materials necessary for the development of the national economy, for the general raising of the standard of living," *Scînteia*, July 6, 1978.

70. *Anuarul Statistic al R.S.R.*, *1982*, 249.

71. Ibid. According to the statistic communiqués, Romanian exports exceeded imports in 1982 by $1.8 billion and in 1983 by $2.4 billion. See *Scînteia*, February 9, 1983, January 29, 1984. See *Review*.

72. *Scînteia*, October 9, 1982.

73. "Dumpingverfahren gegen Ostblock" (Dumping Procedure against the Eastern Bloc) in *Frankfurter Allgemeine Zeitung*, April 6, 1982. Nicolae Ceauşescu himself showed in 1979 that many Romanian products are sold below international prices. *Scînteia*, September 9, 1979.

74. The BAC I-II airplane project was built jointly with British companies, *The Times* (London), June 16, 1978; *Financial Times* (London), March 23, 1983.

75. *Neue Zürcher Zeitung*, May 22, 1980; *Süddeutsche Zeitung*, January 18, 1982.

76. Paul Mentre, *Romania and the IMF* (Study). See RFE-RL, FF005, June 26, 1984; M. R. Jackson, *Romania's Foreign Debt and Its Repayment* (1983), 2; *Frankfurter Allgemeine Zeitung*, April 22, 1982.

77. Wharton, *Review, Part I*, p. 9. See also Jackson, *Romania's Foreign Debt*.

78. In 1980 Romania had a deficit in the balance of payments of $2.4 billion; this decreased to $818 million in 1981. In 1982 the balance had a surplus of $655 million. See Wharton, *Review, Part I*.

79. *Frankfurter Allgemeine Zeitung*, February 17, 1983.

3

Romania's Socialist Agriculture: The Balance Sheet

Paul Grafton

According to official statistics, Romania has more than 3 million people working in agriculture today, which represents some 30 percent of the country's total economically active population. According to the same statistics, the majority of this labor force, namely 2.2 million, are members of the agricultural production cooperatives, the largest sector of socialist agriculture. The other 0.4 million people work in the state sector of agriculture, which is the second component of socialist agriculture. These statistics do not specify the number of private farmers, but the information above indicates that the number of active working people in this private sector is 0.4 million.[1]

Reports in the media show that the socialist transformation of Romania's agriculture had a disruptive impact on the peasant obliged to become either a state employee or member of a cooperative, severing his traditional links with the land; at the same time, the lack of incentives made him apathetic and reluctant to work. An inquiry carried out in 1981 disclosed that about 34 percent of the productive members of the agricultural cooperatives able to work avoided performing any work at all for their cooperative during that year.[2]

Reluctance to work on socialized farms turned out to be so great that the authorities have been forced to mobilize schoolchildren, students, troops, and urban workers to perform work on the land. The number of these substitutes for farm labor increased from year to year, especially after Ceauşescu's rise to power in 1965. Thus the number of substitute workers doubled from 1.5 million in 1979 to 3 million in the fall of 1983, exceeding the entire socialist agricultural labor force of about 2.6 million.[3]

After World War II, Romanian agriculture was visibly modernized and its output grew. From 1950 to 1983 the number of tractors increased from 13,700 to 168,000. During the same period, grain output jumped from 5 million to about 20 million tons.[4] Nevertheless, agricultural efficiency remained poor, leaving Romania at the bottom of the list of countries with similar development, as far as productivity is concerned. Other East European socialist countries generally obtained much better results in agriculture, and a comparison with developed capitalist countries is even more unfavorable for Romania.[5]

The most contradictory aspect of Romania's official agricultural policy is that its primary aim is not to feed the population but is rather to satisfy other economic needs. As a result, by 1981 Romania found itself unable to feed its population adequately, although before the advent of communism it had been called the bread basket of Europe. What is even more surprising is that between the years 1951 to 1981 the population's annual growth was about 1 percent, compared to the agricultural gross output of 4.1 percent, a comfortable margin that could have ensured the supply of food to the population.[6] Moreover, agricultural output remained at a constant high level – annual grain production reached to about 20 million tons between 1980 and 1983 – despite its failure to reach the government's targets.[7] These supplies, however, were exported as a result of an austerity policy designed to reroute substantial quantities of agricultural produce to pay the costs of Romania's industrialization program. President Ceauşescu made it very clear that the RCP gives priority to accumulation over consumption – the rate of accumulation going up from 19.3 percent for the period between 1951–1966 to 33 percent during the years 1966–1980. Between 1967 and 1980 the rate reached its highest level, 36.3 percent.[8]

The most burdensome cost for Romania's industrialization program turned out to be its foreign debts. These debts quintupled between 1976 and 1983, reaching about $10,000 million.[9] The government intends to pay them primarily with agricultural products, because Romania's obsolete and low-quality industrial goods are not competitive on Western markets. For this reason, beef, vegetables, and other agricultural products are being exported rather than sold locally. To pay for two nuclear reactors from Canada, both worth $1,000 million, Romania intends to offer strawberries, wine, leather goods, and textiles in exchange.[10]

Official statistics give either very little or incomplete information on the export of agricultural goods. But even according to inadequate statistics there was an increase of 450 percent in these exports between 1965 and 1981. This included a 17-fold increase in the export of sheep, most likely to Arab oil-producing countries, obviously because of Romania's need to import crude oil from this area.[11] The Romanian media also said that the country exports substantial quantities of agricultural raw materials and products to the Soviet Union to balance its trade with that country, but gives no more details on the nature and extent of these exports.[12]

These exports have seriously disrupted the food supply. After ceasing post-World War II rationing in 1954, when the country's grain output was about 400 kg per capita, Romania resumed it 27 years later, when the output had reached 900 kg per capita. This gives an indication of the extent of Romania's exports, which probably amount to more than 50 percent of its total agricultural output.[13]

The authorities never denied the food shortage; instead, they resumed rationing and increased food prices in 1981 in an attempt to cut public access to a dwindling supply. With the same end in view, they introduced a "scientific" diet for the population that reduced the existing supply of food by 9–15 percent.[14] At the beginning of 1984, the Grand National

Assembly established an extremely modest diet for every citizen, providing annually only about 39 kg of meat and 27 kg of fruit. It is doubtful that even this quantity will be delivered, because the assembly declared that it could be granted only if the plan targets were reached, which seldom happens.[15]

The world economic crisis has had an unfavorable impact on Romania. Agriculture, which in socialist countries is treated as a second class sector of the economy, suffers more than other sectors in this situation. For example, the official media has reported that the fuel quantities to be delivered to the state and collective farms have been reduced in some instances even below the planned figures.[16] Because of the energy crisis, the trend is to return to traditional methods of work, avoiding the use of fuel and energy as much as possible: for example, bed irrigation is recommended over sprinkling, as is the use of horses instead of tractors — the costs of fodder for a pair of horses supposedly amounting to only 150 *lei* daily, whereas a tractor costs some 700 *lei* daily to maintain.[17] The officials also now advocate more use of teams of mowers and reapers, as in the better days of traditional agriculture.[18] They also want to stop the migration of the rural population to the towns, to have more manual workers at their disposal, while at the same time attempting to convince the workers with peasant backgrounds to return to agriculture.[19]

As an innovation to replenish the state's empty stocks and cover the burdensome payments of foreign debts, the authorities have turned again to the private sector, insisting that it should provide the state with about 20 percent, or more, of its agricultural output. According to the most recent data available (1981), on comparable plots of land, the productivity of the private farmer is 4.83 times higher than the socialist sector in fruit production, 3.05 times higher in livestock production, 1.94 times higher in milk production, and 1.14 times higher in grain output. This explains why in 1981 private agriculture, while representing about 15 percent of the country's agricultural land, produced about 60 percent of the country's milk output, 60 percent of its eggs, 60 percent of its fruit, 47 percent of its wool, 44 percent of its meat, 40 percent of its grapes and 14 percent of its grain. In fact, it has managed to supply the country with very significant amounts of food over a long period.[20]

It is doubtful that the peasants will respond to the party's appeal and increase their output, unless the government stops the very low price system it has established and allows a return to a market-oriented one. A genuine revival of Romanian agriculture is likely to occur only when farmers are given incentives. So far this is precisely what the Communist party has not been able to provide, and this policy will probably not change in the near future.

Notes

1. *Anuarul Statistic al RSR, 1982*, pp. 60, 131–134; *Scînteia*, January 29, 1984, "Comunicatul Indeplinirii Planului de Stat pe 1983" (Communiqué on the Fulfillment of the 1983 State Plan).

2. *Revista Economica*, no. 51, (December 18, 1981).

3. *Scînteia*, March 8, 1979, May 7, 1980; *Scînteia Tineretului*, October 29, 1983; *Anuarul Statistic al RSR, 1982*, pp. 60, 131–134.

4. Ibid., 116–187; *Scînteia*, January 29, 1984. These sources of information also give the following data on the modernization of agriculture:

	1950	1983
Area provided with irrigation (in hectares)	42,500	2,500,300
Chemical fertilizers employed in agriculture (in tons)	5,900	1,373,000

and the following increase in agricultural output:

	1950	1983
Fruit production (in million tons)	0.4	2.0
Fresh vegetables (in million tons)	1.1	4.3
Meat production (in million tons)	0.7	1.5

5. *Anuarul Statistic al RSR, 1982*, pp. 354, 356 shows that in 1980 Romania obtained 2,840 kg of wheat per hectare, while Yugoslavia obtained 3,350 kg, Bulgaria 3,970 kg, the GDR 4,380 kg, Czechoslovakia 4,500 kg, and Hungary 4,760 kg. According to the same source of information, Romania also obtained poor results in the number of cattle per 100 hectares of agricultural land. Thus, in the same year it obtained 46 head per 100 hectares, while Poland obtained 61, Czechoslovakia 77 and the GDR 95. Of course, a comparison with developed countries is still more unfavorable for Romania. Thus, in the same year Holland obtained 253 head of cattle per 100 hectares.

6. *Viitorul Social,* (The Social Future) (January/February 1981), 13–14; *Anuarul Statistic al RSR, 1982*, 22–23; *Anuarul Statistic al RSR, 1982*, 42.

7. Ibid., 138; *Scînteia*, January 29, 1984, "Communiqué on the Fulfillment of the 1983 State Plan."

8. *Scînteia*, December 24, 1980. In his speech to the plenum of the National Council of the Socialist Democracy and Unity Front, Nicolae Ceaușescu said: "History has kept not what was consumed [by a people], but what was accumulated." Ibid., June 2, 1980. In his speech to the RCP Central Committee plenum Ceaușescu also said in this respect, " . . . for the future of a people what is decisive is not the amount of [their] consumption, but the amount of [their] accumulation." *Agerpres*, February 28, 1984; *Anuarul Statistic al RSR, 1982*, 49.

9. RFER, *Romanian Situation Report*, no. 23 (November 11, 1981), item 2; no. 11 (June 29, 1983), item 2.

10. Ibid., no. 16 (September 16, 1983), item 6; *Scînteia*, February 8, 1984.

11. Calculated on the basis of the *Anuarul Statistic al RSR, 1982*, p. 269.

12. *Revista Economică*, no. 6 (February 10, 1984), F. Magereanu's item.

13. *Scînteia*, October 10, 1981; RFER, *Romanian Situation Report*, no. 23 (November 11, 1981), item 2.

14. *Scînteia*, July 14, 1982, 2–3, "Programul de Alimentatie Stiintifica a Populatiei," (The Program for the Scientific Alimentation of the Population), RFER, *Romanian Situation Report*, no. 14, (August 4, 1982), item no. 3.

15. *Scînteia*, December 17, 1983; *Buletinul Oficial al Republicii Socialiste România*, (The Official Bulletin of the Socialist Re-

public Romania), no. 97 (December 19, 1983); Hotarirea No. 8 a Marii Adunari Nationale (The Decision No. 8 of the Grand National Assembly), RFER, *Romanian Situation Report*, no. 1 (January 7, 1984), item no. 1.

16. *România Libera*, April 27, 1983; *Scînteia*, May 10, 1983.

17. *Scînteia*, December 10, 1983, Ceauşescu's speech to the RCP Central Committee conference on agricultural problems; *Agricultura Socialistă*, February 2, 1980.

18. *Radio Bucureşti*, July 25, 1983.

19. *Scînteia*, February 19, 1984, praises the return of a construction worker to the countryside to work as a peasant.

20. Calculated on the basis of the *Anuarul Statistic al RSR, 1982*, 120–179.

4

Romania and its Allies

George Ciorănescu

According to the classical notion of alliance, Romania's allies are the members of the 1955 Warsaw Pact (the Soviet Union, Bulgaria, Czechoslovakia, Hungary, Poland, and, originally, Albania, which withdrew from the organization in 1968). In modern terms, an alliance implies not only active military cooperation but also close political cooperation. Because one of the Warsaw Pact participants, the Soviet Union, is a superpower, it holds a ruling position vis-à-vis the other members, the small and middle-sized states, whose national economies and defense systems are, to a great extent, subordinate to Moscow. The Warsaw Pact was in fact set up as the main link in a chain to strengthen Soviet domination over its satellites. To this day Moscow has succeeded in maintaining its initial goal of economic, political, and military integration of its Communist allies.

Generally, there have been no dramatic developments in the bilateral relations between Romania and its secondary Warsaw Pact allies. Good relations have been strained only in those instances when Moscow allowed or encouraged it. Accordingly, Romania's relations with the Soviet Union, the Warsaw Pact, and the CMEA as a whole has determined to a great extent its bilateral relations with the other members of the alliance.

Over the last 40 years, Romania's links with the Soviet Union have changed from full subordination to comparative independence, with Romania gradually regaining in part its economic, political, and military sovereignty. Until 1960, the Communist regime of Romania had totally accepted the Soviet Union's foreign policy. It did not deviate from the line set down by the Kremlin and was one of the USSR's most loyal satellites. In its domestic, economic, and social policies, Romania followed the Soviet model, and Romania's foreign policy was determined by its East European treaties of friendship and mutual assistance, as well as by long-term economic treaties with the other Communist states. Romania's obedience was demonstrated in 1948 when Gheorghiu-Dej, obeying orders from Moscow, condemned Tito in an inflammatory address, entitled "The Yugoslav Communist Party under the Influence of Murderers and Spies."

Regaining Economic Autonomy

Since 1960, Romania's image as a loyal Soviet satellite has been gradually superseded as it has rejected more and more openly the policy of subordination to a central power and has advocated cooperation among equal socialist allies instead. The Moscow Declaration of the International Conference of the Communist Parties in November 1960, which — as a solution for the Sino-Soviet split — formally admitted that all Communist parties are equal and sovereign, allowed Romania to assert its economic independence, which involved less of a risk that the Soviet Union would react drastically than would the assertion of political or military autonomy.[1] At first, Romania confined itself to claiming the right to build its own metallurgical industry by constructing a major complex at Galati. The principle it invoked to support its claim was valid from the socialist point of view, because Lenin himself had talked about the priority of the development of the metallurgical industry.

At this time, however, Nikita Khrushchev, eager to turn the CMEA into an instrument for integration of the Eastern bloc, was planning to endow it with a supranational planning body capable of forcing Soviet allies to plan tasks corresponding to the international division of labor. Because this division assigned to Romania the role of an agrarian state and purveyor of raw materials, Romania's plans for industrialization were not welcome.

Romania, differing from its socialist allies in its April 1964 Declaration, rejected the idea of remaining an agricultural state and of allowing an international body to control its economy, arguing that this "would turn sovereignty into a meaningless notion." The management of the economy should be left to the Romanian state, for "the planned management of national economy is one of the fundamental, essential, and inalienable attributes of the sovereignty of a socialist state."[2]

Under Leonid Brezhnev, the Soviet Union twice tried to resume its 1962 integrationist strategy, in 1971 at the twenty-fifth session of the CMEA in Bucharest, when a comprehensive program was adopted, and again in 1975, at a CMEA plenary meeting in Budapest, when a plan of measures for mutual integration was adopted.[3] In the meantime, however, the idea of Romanian specialization in agriculture had been attenuated somewhat. The CMEA had accepted the possibility of Romania's developing some industry, although they remained reluctant to accept Romania's pursuance of a multilateral economic policy. At the same time, Romania had become more open to economic integration because of the oil crisis, which forced Romania to depend on the Soviet Union for the oil and raw materials it needed for the achievement of its ambitious plans. Nevertheless, even under these circumstances, Romania has refused to make any major concessions to the Soviet pressures, always responding by making some insignificant concessions but rejecting and denouncing the principle of supranational domination.

Romania's stand has been consistent both at the CMEA meetings, when the problem of changing the structure of the organization was raised, and in articles about socialist theory published by the Romanian press.[4] Under present conditions Romania is helped because more CMEA members, such as Hungary, are now against a central planning body. The final documents adopted by the CMEA's June 1984 summit meeting – the first in 15 years – mentioned classic Romanian foreign policy principles: the respect for state sovereignty, independence, and national interest as the principles of international socialism. Romania also did not take any further steps toward the economic integration advocated by the Soviet Union.[5]

Nevertheless, the dispute between the partisans of economic integration and economic sovereignty continues. In speeches at RCP Central Committee meetings in July and October of 1982, Ceauşescu admitted that Romania's policy of industrialization had been taken to task both within the ranks of the RCP and by some socialist countries. He argued, however, that without the development of industry Romania could never make progress nor defend its national integrity.

Regaining Foreign Policy Autonomy

The most interesting part of the April 1964 Declaration was Romania's statement about relations among the Communist parties and states, taking a stand against the establishment of any supranational authority in the socialist camp that would enforce its solutions upon the member countries. It emphasized that no one – meaning the Soviet Union – has the right to impose its own experience upon the other Communist countries. In this way a rejoinder was given to another project of Khrushchev's, which was set forth in Budapest on April 3, 1964, to further foreign policy cooperation among the Communist countries to strengthen the unity of the Communist camp.[6]

The Soviet Union

The publication of the Romanian Declaration apparently had not been inspired by fervent patriotism; unfriendly personal relations were more likely to have accounted for it. As far back as 1957, in order to de-Stalinize the Communist leadership of Eastern Europe, Khrushchev had planned to replace Gheorghiu-Dej with Iosif Chisinevschi and Miron Constantinescu, who were considered more pro-Khrushchev than liberal.[7] The tension between Gheorghiu-Dej and Khrushchev reached a critical point between 1963 and 1964, when Khrushchev not only once again threatened to unseat Gheorghiu-Dej but made an even graver threat: to dismember the Romanian state. In the summer of 1963, it was rumored in Budapest that the Hungarian-Romanian border was going to be revised in Hungary's favor.[8] Faced with this Romania replied by raising the issue of Bessarabia, the Romanian territory annexed by the Soviet Union after World War II, to point out that the Soviet Union did not have the moral right to act as an arbiter in minority issues, because it had itself annexed a territory in which Romanians made up the vast majority of the indigenous population.

The discussion about Bessarabia went beyond the Romanian-Soviet framework when Mao Zedong unexpectedly stepped in on the Romanian side, declaring that the Soviet Union had unjustly occupied Bessarabia and Northern Bucovina.[9] Now, Romania could rely on the authority of Karl Marx, who had claimed, among other things, that the 1812 transfer of Bessarabia from Turkey to Russia had had no judicial basis, since the Sublime Porte had ceded a territory that did not belong to it but above all had belonged and still belonged to Moldavia.[10]

The escalation of the Bessarabian issue was halted when Ceaușescu paid an official visit to Soviet Moldavia in August 1976 – a visit considered a conciliatory gesture toward the USSR. While the Romanians were toning down their polemical debate with the Soviets about Bessarabia, Ceaușescu and Hungarian leader Janos Kadar reached an agreement that the problem of minorities was to be considered a domestic one. The Hungarian minority in Romania and the Romanian minority in Hungary were to serve as a bridge between the two peoples.[11]

Another Soviet project, instigated by Professor E. B.

Valev, represented a second threat to dismember Romania. In 1964 Professor Valev had published an article advocating that an international production complex be set up on the Lower Danube, on territories detached from Romania, Bulgaria, and the Soviet Union. Romania was supposed to contribute two-thirds of its national territory and three-fourths of its population to this complex. Practically speaking, that meant the dismantling of Romania as a sovereign entity. The Romanian protest against the Valev project appeared in an article in *Viata Economica*. The debate ended when *Izvestia* raised its own criticism of the Valev project.[12]

The dispute between Gheorghiu-Dej and Khrushchev unexpectedly ended in victory for the Romanian, who managed to stay in power and did not give in to attempts to dismember his country. Gheorghiu-Dej also was gratified when the charges brought by Mikhail Suslov against Khrushchev included three counts of indictment related to the latter's policy toward Romania. Gheorghiu-Dej had a right to believe that he had to some extent contributed to the ousting of Khrushchev from his position as first secretary of the CPSU.

The tension between Romania and its allies, which had twice collectively condemned Romanian diplomatic actions, reached a culminating point in the summer of 1968 during the Czechoslovakian crisis. Romania saw in Alexander Dubcek's Czechoslovakia the possibility of a genuine ally, at least in establishing a joint front opposed to Soviet hegemony. In August 1968, President Ceauşescu visited Czechoslovakia, where he signed a treaty of friendship and mutual assistance, recalling the right of each state to establish its own policy without any outside intervention. When Czechoslovakia was invaded on August 20–21, 1968, Romania did not join in the collective action of its allies because it was afraid that a similar action might be taken against Romania as well. The government even went so far as to protest against its socialist allies' actions in public meetings, which, at times, displayed anti-Soviet sentiments.[13]

Following the Soviet intervention in Czechoslovakia, first secretary Leonid Brezhnev delivered a speech at the fifth Polish United Workers Party congress on November 12, 1968 in which he elaborated on the doctrine, which bore his name, that spelled out that the sovereignty of the Warsaw Pact countries was to be limited by the right of the Soviet government to intervene in their domestic affairs whenever the interests of the Communist party were jeopardized.

Although during Brezhnev's rule the Soviet Union continued to claim the leading role in the Communist world movement and the validity of Soviet experience as a universal model, there was no opportunity to apply the Brezhnev doctrine until the events in Poland in 1980. On that occasion, the Brezhnev doctrine was put into practice on the grounds that the action of the trade union, Solidarity, endangered a basic Marxist-Leninist principle – the hegemony of the Communist party.

Romania's response to the events in Poland was far more moderate than that of its Communist allies. It emphasized that the Polish developments were primarily the concern of Poland and that the Polish government, party, and people should be allowed to solve their own problems independently, according to the principle of noninterference.[14]

Not long ago, when the Soviet first secretary, Yuri Andropov, tried to bring Romania close to the Soviet Union, the CMEA, and the Warsaw Pact, he reiterated the Brezhnev doctrine, adding new arguments. Andropov claimed that modern production and the increasing antagonism between East and West demand the integration of socialist countries and a reduction of their individual prerogatives. Romania's response to the Soviets was that the process of merging nations should not be imposed from without but rather accomplished by voluntary acceptance.

Personal relations between Ceauşescu and Andropov had started under unfavorable auspices. In fact, according to President Richard Nixon, Ceauşescu had not counted on the election of Andropov as Brezhnev's successor, speculating that Andropov had made too many enemies while he was head of the KGB. On top of that, the few meetings Ceauşescu had with Andropov were not particularly cordial. At their first meeting, which took place after Brezhnev's funeral, Andropov emphasized to the Romanian secretary general that no change could be made in the Balkans without Andropov's assent.[15] Later on, at the meeting of the Consultative Committee of the Warsaw Pact in January 1983 in Prague and June 1983 in Moscow, divergencies of opinion appeared between the two leaders with respect to closer cooperation within the Eastern bloc military organization as well as the Euromissiles issue. Very likely, a more open clash was postponed because of Yuri Andropov's death.

In this tense atmosphere, the short visit of several hours Ceauşescu paid to Konstantin Chernenko, the new Soviet general secretary, on June 4, 1984 was anticipated with great interest. It was the first official visit of the Romanian general secretary to the Soviet Union in 14 years and was designed to smooth out Soviet-Romanian differences and to ensure that the CMEA summit scheduled for June 12, 1984 could go ahead without major problems. Apparently neither side changed its previous stand on the basic problems, Tass noting that the talks were "frank," which in Soviet rhetoric means that both sides differ on many issues, while *Scînteia* on June 20, 1984 underlined that it is inevitable for different opinions and viewpoints to occur.

The People's Republic of China

The qualitative change in the links between Romania and the Soviet Union would not have been possible without the active support of China, which created an atmosphere favorable to the appearance of autonomist movements in the Communist camp. China openly opposed Moscow's hegemonism and threatened to polarize around it any rebellious Communist countries. Romania understood from the very beginning the potential for exploiting the divergent attitudes of Moscow and Beijing — not merely exchanging one suzerain for another. In this way, Romania succeeded in becoming the only Warsaw Pact member to enjoy both party-to-party relations with China and extensive military cooperation. If one accepts Albanian First Secretary Enver Hoxha's hypothesis, Romania and China may even be allies, linked by a secret agreement signed in 1970, during a visit to China by Ion Ionita, who was Romania's minister of defense at the time.[16]

Romania drew closer to China slowly and cautiously. Beginning in 1960, when the Sino-Soviet confrontation flared up at the RCP Third Congress on June 22–26, 1960, Romania noted that there were differences of opinion between Beijing and Moscow regarding the unity of the Communist camp and the Communist policy of economic development. The Moscow Conference of November 1960 confirmed these differences between the two major powers. In August 1962, Chinese Foreign Minister Chen Y hinted for the first time at the possibility that the principles of equality established at the Moscow Conference could be applied to the Romanian situation. This was reiterated later in a Chinese text, dated June 14, 1963, that discussed the chauvinist tendencies of a major power, which wanted to enforce its will upon others under the pretext of the international division of labor.[17]

In 1964, encouraged by the importance conferred on Romania by China, Romania acted as an arbiter between Moscow and Beijing, calling on the Soviets to stop publishing Suslov's anti-Chinese indictments and on the Chinese to stop their press attacks directed at the Soviet Union. Although this attempt at mediation was not successful, it did represent another step by Romania to involve itself actively in Asian affairs.

Romania's relations with China could not be maintained at that level for long because, in exchange for its promise to support Romania's independence and sovereignty, Beijing wanted Romania to fall in line with Chinese policy. Chinese Foreign Minister Zhou En-lai had made this request during his visit to Romania in June 1966, when he spoke about the need to oppose modern revisionism, meaning the Soviet Union. When Romania refused to align itself with the aggressively anti-Soviet policy advocated by China, the two countries could not find the appropriate wording for a final communiqué upon Zhou's departure.

In 1970, China acquired new international stature by normalizing its diplomatic relations with the United States and being accepted at the United Nations and, thus, had no more need for Romania's mediation with the Soviet Union. Diplomatic visits between the two continued at various levels, however, with routine declarations and assurances concerning China's support in the struggle waged by the Romanian people against foreign intervention. In the wake of Romania's catastrophic floods in 1970, China made a substantial loan to rebuild the Romanian economy, which the Soviet Union had refused to do.

High level Chinese visitors reappeared in Romania with the visits of Premier Hua Guofeng in August 1978 and Communist Party leader Hu Yaobang in May 1983. The Soviet Union, of course, did not welcome Chinese-made Romanian gun boats cruising on the Black Sea, nor the idea of a Chinese consulate opening at Constanta, from which the Chinese could keep track of the movements of Soviet ships on the Black Sea. China also approved of Romania's stand on Euro-missiles during Romanian Premier Constantin Dascalescu's visit to China in November 1983, while Romanian policy in Asia also supported the Chinese line.[18] Even if China is not a formal ally of Romania, since 1960 China has been a counterbalance to the Soviet Union's attempts to limit Romanian autonomy, which could never have been maintained by Romania without the moral and material support from within the Communist bloc.

Yugoslavia

As far back as 1962, Romania found another source of support in its struggle to detach itself from the Soviet Union, namely in Yugoslavia, a nation much closer than China. Romania was able to normalize its relations with Yugoslavia only after the Soviet-Yugoslav Declaration was signed in Belgrade in 1955, putting an end to the Soviet-Yugoslav conflict. In June 1963, an important Romanian-Yugoslav agreement was signed to construct the Iron Gates I hydroelectric power station, which called for a substantial investment on Romania's part at a time when it had refused to take a greater part in the investment pool schemes of the CMEA. Shortly after this agreement was signed, Gheorghiu-Dej paid a spectacular visit to Yugoslavia and was given a warm reception and honors far exceeding those given to Khrushchev earlier that year.

Under these circumstances, Romania's April 1964 Declaration was welcomed by Yugoslavia, which espoused similar ideas. As was the case with China, some observers of Balkan affairs assumed that after 1968 Romania and Yugoslavia formed a secret defensive alliance. In any case, Romania continues to maintain close relations with both Yugoslavia and China in every field. There are periodic meetings between Romanian and Yugoslav leaders, which have continued even after Tito's death. Economic cooperation has been extended to military matters in the form of the joint production of the fighter plane, the Orao, a venture that contradicts the principle of standardization of armaments within the Warsaw Pact.

Since Yugoslavia has been associated with the CMEA, it has held similar views and often actively supported Romania within the organization. Yugoslavia also favored the projects involving Balkan cooperation advanced by Romania in 1957 and in 1969 that were aimed at stabilizing the situation in the Balkans and possibly at ensuring the security of Romania's southern frontier. Romania's Balkan projects were not looked upon favorably by Bulgaria, however, which has restricted itself to the role of faithful ally and interpreter of Moscow's wishes.

China had allegedly encouraged a special project in the Balkans involving an alliance between Romania, Yugoslavia, and Albania, which supposedly was presented by Zhou in 1966 to Albanian Defense Minister Bequir Balluku. It did not find the approval of Enver Hoxha, however, who preferred not to link his "correct" policy with the "adventurous policy of Titoists and the Romanian revisionists." Nevertheless, Hoxha added that, were Romania to be attacked by the Soviet Union, Albania would hasten to defend it, provided the Romanians defend themselves and that neither NATO, nor any individual NATO member came to its aid.[19]

Although Romania has not let itself be influenced by Yugoslavia's domestic political system, which is more liberal than its own, its cooperation with Yugoslavia in the field of foreign policy has continued along the lines initially set. In addition, the two nations also cooperate with respect to relations with nonaligned and developing countries. Romania has even tried to modify its self-defined status as a socialist country to that of a socialist developing country, enabling it to reinforce its solidarity with the Third World, while alienating it even more from the Warsaw Pact.

Albania

Romania has rather strange diplomatic relations with the small rebellious ally, Albania, which withdrew from the Warsaw Pact in 1968. Although Romania does not maintain any party-to-party relations, it does have state-to-state diplomatic links with Tirana, which are characterized by Hoxha as "cold, stale, tasteless and unpleasant." In 1961, Romania and the other Warsaw Pact member countries withdrew their ambassadors to Tirana, then, rather unexpectedly, Romania sent one back two years later. To normalize party-to-party relations, Hoxha has demanded that the RCP publicly acknowledge mistakes the RCP has made about the Albanian Communist Party. The Albanians do not conceal their scorn for the RCP and its leaders, whom Hoxha considers to be political puppets. In the opinion of the Albanian periodical, *Zeri i Populit*, neutral Communist parties such as the RCP are ruled by cliques of bourgeois intellectuals, who play on anti-Soviet sentiments and whose foreign policy is oriented toward Yugoslavia and the capitalist countries. According to Hoxha, Gheorghiu-Dej was only a puppet for Khrushchev, "who thought that he had Dej in his waistcoat pocket like the small ivory knife which he would bring out and toy with at meetings."

Hoxha has characterized Ceauşescu as an adventurous bourgeois revisionist and equated Ceauşescu's domestic policy with bankruptcy and corruption, accusing him of buying and selling on the foreign market only to gain percentages and medals for himself. Hoxha added that the anti-Sovietism of Romania's policy of independence vis-à-vis Moscow is only a show as long as Romania remains a member of the Warsaw Pact and the CMEA.[20]

Regaining National Defense Autonomy

The Romanian military doctrine, according to which national defense and the organization and leadership of the armed forces are a prerogative of a sovereign state, was long in the making. It was not drafted until after the invasion of Czechoslovakia in 1968 and took on a consistent form only in 1972.[21] The reason is that expressing opinions on military matters that differ from those of the Soviet Union involves higher risks for Romania than claiming sovereign control over its own economy and foreign policy.

As early as 1965, the relations between Romania and the Warsaw Pact suffered a crisis similar to that which had taken place between 1962 and 1964 within the CMEA. This crisis was precipitated by Leonid Brezhnev who suggested a political strengthening of the Pact in a speech on September 14, 1965. This provoked an indirect reply from Romania, which demanded that the tactical nuclear missiles, located on the territory of Soviet allies, be placed under the joint control of the Soviet Union and of the Warsaw Pact member countries, a condition unacceptable to the Soviet Union.

When Moscow persisted, the RCP gave a reply even more drastic than that of Gheorghiu-Dej in 1964, declaring that the existence of the military blocs had become "an anachronism inconsistent with the national independence and sovereignty of the peoples." This caused some to suppose that, if need be, Romania was ready to pull out of the Warsaw pact.

Another critical time came in the summer of 1968, when

Romania did not join in the Warsaw Pact invasion of Czecho-slovakia. It had not even been invited to attend the Dresden, Moscow, and Bratislava planning meetings prior to the invasion, because of its open support of the Dubcek regime. President Ceauşescu thereupon declared publicly that it was inconceivable that the national independence of a socialist state could be violated by other socialist states, and, in the wake of the military invasion of Czechoslovakia, Romania began setting up paramilitary units that could mobilize the country's able-bodied population in the case of conflict with the Soviet Union.[22]

In the same year (1968) another grave crisis arose between Bucharest and the Warsaw Pact, when the Political Consultative Committee of the Pact met in Moscow. The committee discussed some aspects of the unified command system, as well as the aid to be offered to Vietnam for its impending invasion of Kampuchea and the increase in the defense spending of the Warsaw Pact members. Back in Bucharest after the meeting in Moscow, Ceauşescu made it clear that Romania's military force would serve only under a Romanian command, that it considered the Warsaw Pact organization a simple defense pact, and that Romania had no intention of increasing its military spending, but, on the contrary, planned to make cuts.[23] The principle of sovereignty in matters of national defense was clearly reemphasized.

Later, in 1972, the Organization of the National Defense law formally declared that "the right to make decisions about matters of defense is a sovereign prerogative of the Romanian state," and Romania's defense would be reorganized toward "every horizon," implying that it was directed against all of Romania's neighbors – all Warsaw Pact allies, except for Yugoslavia.[24]

In 1974, the tension between Romania and the Soviet Union heightened again, when Bucharest objected to the construction of a railway line on its territory that would facilitate the quick transfer of Soviet troops to Bulgaria. As good allies, the Romanians had permitted a token number of Soviet troops to cross the Romanian border under the supervision of Romanian escorts in armored vehicles. As a result, in 1978 the Soviet Union was forced to open a four-ship ferry service between Ilichevsk in the USSR and Varna, Bulgaria. Each ship was able to carry about 150 tanks or railway wagons and several thousand troops.

Finally, in 1983, Romania again differed from its Pact allies with respect to the acute issue of nuclear missiles in Europe. In a speech delivered on May 26, Ceauşescu compared "the present nuclear threat to that posed by the seditious Nero," without specifying whether President Ronald Reagan or the Soviet First Secretary Andropov was being likened to the Roman emperor. This attitude is in accordance with the disarmament policy advocated by Romania as far back as 1965, when it voted at the United Nations in favor of the establishment of a denuclearized zone in Latin America, while the other Soviet bloc countries abstained. Romania also broke unity with the Communist bloc in 1983 when it supported the Japanese view that missiles dismantled in Europe should not be moved to Asia.[25]

Although the options suggested by Romania in the messages to President Reagan and First Secretary Andropov were more favorable to Moscow than to Washington, nevertheless, unlike its allies, Romania took to task not only the U.S. but also the Soviet stand and urged the countries on whose territories nuclear missiles were to be sited, such as Czechoslovakia and East Germany, not to accept them.[26]

Ceauşescu's avoidance of a September 1983 meeting with Marshal Viktor Kulikov, commander in chief of the Warsaw Pact Armed Forces, as well as his dispatch of Minister of Defense C. Olteanu to Beijing immediately after Kulikov's departure, was probably due to Soviet pressure on Romania to accept the Warsaw Pact position on the missiles problem.

Romania's stand on its sovereign right to decide on matters of national defense has resulted in the odd situation in which a founding member of the Warsaw Pact has not allowed its allies to hold maneuvers on its territory since 1962 and has limited its involvement in joint exercises and maneuvers on the territories of its allies to staff officers and map exercises since 1969. Its strategy differs from that of its allies. It has formulated defense plans to protect itself from its own allies. It has its own armaments, which are mainly produced domestically or are imported from the West – in contravention of the manditory standardization rule in force among the allies of the Warsaw Pact. And, finally, it often adopts political stands in military matters of joint interest that differ from those of its allies.

Conclusions

Over the last 40 years, Romania's policy toward its allies has fluctuated greatly. More often than not, Romania has taken an entirely different position from the rest of the Soviet bloc. On the one hand, Romania has adopted flexible tactics by resisting the total economic and military integration of the Communist bloc – which was chiefly pursued by the Soviet Union and, to some extent, by the other members of the alliance. But, at the same time, Romania has remained part of the CMEA and the Warsaw Pact.

Romania has adopted an independent stand, breaking with the other members of the Warsaw Pact, in a number of foreign policy matters. Beyond Romania's decision to resume diplomatic ties with West Germany and maintain its relations with Israel, at the United Nations it has expressed points of view differing from those of its Communist allies. Also during the 1983 Conference on Security and Cooperation in Europe held in Madrid, Romania not only differed from its allies in the General Assembly, but also tried to have its own representatives in the work committees in addition to those sent by the Warsaw Pact, NATO, and the nonaligned countries. Ceauşescu himself condemned the "brutal cynicism" of the violation of Kampuchea's sovereignty and territorial integrity and stressed that the principle of nonintervention, indispensable to the independence and freedom of all nations, had been flouted in Afghanistan.

Relations between the Bucharest regime and its allies

were not likely to change with Konstantin Chernenko as secretary general of the Communist Party of the Soviet Union. In Chernenko's first speech delivered to the Soviet Central Committee on February 13, 1984, the new secretary general, who turned out to be an orthodox and conservative Communist, expressed his readiness to continue the East European policy of his predecessors, Andropov and Brezhnev, declaring that he would develop and strengthen "a comprehensive cohesion and cooperation of all countries of the socialist community in every field." Shortly before the change in leadership in the Kremlin, a strong Soviet delegation led by Andrei Gromyko visited Romania between January 30 and February 1, 1984. It failed to obtain any major concessions from the Bucharest regime, either regarding more cohesion within the Warsaw Pact and the CMEA or on the Euromissiles issue.

In the spring of 1984, Romania again took the opportunity to dissociate itself from other Communist countries by deciding to attend the 1984 Olympic Games in Los Angeles, despite the Soviet Union's boycott of the games and similar announcements from Moscow's loyal allies that followed subsequently. Bucharest's decision went far beyond the limits of sportsmanship and was clearly a political act. Although the president of the Romanian National Olympic Committee denied that the Soviet Union had pressured Romania to join the boycott, it can be assumed that the Kremlin was disturbed by the Romanian decision, taken at a moment of international tension, when Moscow needed to present to the free world a united Communist front.

Nevertheless, Ceauşescu's June 1984 visit to the Soviet Union ended with an agreement on more stable economic relations, and Romania promised to adopt a more constructive attitude at the CMEA's future meetings. Under the Romanian-Soviet agreement of July 18, 1984, Romania is to provide the labor force and the infrastructure for natural gas drilling and production in Turkmenistan, while receiving natural gas deliveries in return. As announced by Radio Moscow, about 3,000 Romanian workers will be employed in the natural gas fields of Central Asia. The wish to strengthen Romania's relations with the CMEA was also expressed by Prime Minister Dascalescu at the meeting held in Havana in November 1984.

Last, but not least, Ceauşescu announced at the thirteenth party congress in November 1984 that his country is prepared to accept the extension of the Warsaw Pact treaty due to expire in 1985. At the same time, the RCP also announced its acceptance of the Soviet plan for an international Communist conference.

The acceptance of these Soviet positions does not mean, however, that the Romanians have given up their autonomous stand. Even after Ceauşescu's visit to Moscow, for example, differences of opinion with the Soviet Union emerged. The Romanian mass media continued to avoid such key words as "socialist integration," while news leaked from official circles made clear that Romania had agreed to extend the Warsaw Pact treaty only after being given guarantees that no military maneuvers would take place on Romanian soil. Basic differences also exist between Moscow and Bucharest on the projected international conference of Communist parties, which is viewed by the Soviets as a means of enforcing their grip over the parties, but in which the Romanians are willing to participate only if it remains purely a forum for the exchange of ideas.

Romania's geographic position—exposing it to the constant pressure of a neighboring superpower and surrounding it, with the exception of Yugoslavia, by neighbors loyal to Moscow—does not always allow it to differ from the bloc or to alienate itself entirely from it. In fact, because of its lack of military power as compared with that of the USSR, Romania's independence is, for the most part, merely theoretical. Nevertheless, for at least the last 20 years Romania has always rejected the need for centralized Communist control and a unified economic and social model.

In a 1983 Vienna speech, after emphasizing the existence of the difference between Romania's foreign policy and that of its allies faithful to Moscow, U.S. Vice President George Bush called on U.S. policy to differentiate between the various member states of the Communist bloc, adding that Bucharest should be supported in its attempt to detach itself from the Communist alliance. Romania's position vis-à-vis Moscow and its allies should thus neither be viewed as one of absolute sovereignty nor of complete obedience to Moscow, as in Stalin's time. From the Western point of view, Romania's semiautonomous status represents at least a weak point in the otherwise monolithic structure of the Warsaw Pact, as well as an opportunity to have some influence on the policy of the bloc.

Unfortunately, as long as Romania's foreign policy is not matched by a domestic policy that observes the national interests it claims to represent, it cannot be appreciated by the Romanian people, and Romania will remain unattractive as a model for the other subordinate members of the Communist alliance.

Notes

1. Declaraţia Consfătuirii Reprezentanţilor Partedelor Comuniste şi Muncitoreşti" (Declaration of the Conference of Communist and workers Parties' Representatives), Scînteia, December 4, 1960.

2. "Declaraţia cu Privire la Poziţia Partidului Muncitoresc Român in Problemele Miscării Comuniste şi Muncitoresti Internationale Adoptată de Plenara Largită a CC al PMR din Aprilie 1964" (Declaration Concerning Romanian Workers Party on Communist and Workers International Movement Problems, Adopted by the Plenary Meeting of the RWP in April 1964), Scînteia, April 26, 1964.

3. Romanian Media Call for Comecon Aid to Less Developed Members and Oppose Supernational Schemes, RFER, Background Report, no. 92 (June 5, 1975) (Romania); Harry Trend, Backdrop for the 29th Comecon Council Session, RFE Report no. 105 (June, 16, 1975) (Eastern Europe); RFER, Romanian Situation Reports, No.s 22, 26, 36, 41, and 45, from June 13, July 11, September 18, October 23, November 20, 1975.

4. J. F. Brown, Thirty Years of Comecon, RFER, Background Report, no. 8 (January 12, 1979) (Eastern Europe); Patrick Moore,

Romania and Comecon: Oil and Independence, RFER, *Background Report*, no. 135 (June 18, 1979) (Romania); Cam Hudson, *The 35th CMEA Session Meeting at a Time of Uncertainty*, RFER, *Background Report*, no. 182 (June 29, 1981) (Eastern Europe); Cam Hudson, *The CMEA at the Crossroads: But Which Ones?* RFER, *Background Report*, no. 134 (June 15, 1982).

    5. Comecon summit statements, Tass, June 15, 1984.

    6. *Archiv der Gegenwart* 34 (Bonn, Vienna, Zurich: Siegler & Co. K.G., 1964):11–163.

    7. Robert R. King, *History of the Romanian Communist Party*, (Stanford, Calif.: Hoover Institution Press, 1980), 94; Gheorghe Gheorghiu-Dej, "Dare de Seamă a Delegatiei Partidului Munictoresc Român la cel de-al III-lea Congres al P.C.U.S" (Report of the Romanian Workers Party to the SUCP XXII Congress), *Scînteia*, December 7, 1961.

    8. Paul Underwood, "Rumors of Soviet Pullout Buoy Hungarian Hopes," *New York Times*, July 23, 1963.

    9. Mao Tse-tung, "Interview with the Japanese Socialist," in Dennis J. Doolin, *Territorial Claims in the Sino-Soviet Conflict* (Stanford, Calif.: Stanford University Press, 1965), 42–44; George Ciorănescu, "Revirement Politique," in *Aspects des Relations Russo-Roumaines. Retrospective, et Orientations*, (Paris: Minard, 1967), 227–239.

    10. Karl Marx, *Insemnări despre Români* (Notes on Romanians), Andrei Otetea and S. Schwann, eds. (Bucharest: Editura Academiei, 1964).

    11. Romanian-Hungarian Joint Communiqué, *Scînteia*, June 17, 1977; RFER, *Romanian Situation Report*, no. 20, June 22, 1977.

    12. E. B. Valev, "Problemele Dezvoltarii Economice a Raioanelor Dunărene din România, Bulgaria şi USSR" (The Problems of the Economic Development of the Danubian Districts of Romania, Bulgaria, and the Soviet Union), *Viaţa Economică*, no. 24 (June 5, 1964), 5–14; "Concepţii Potrivnice Principiilor de Bază Dintre Ţările Socialist" (Notions Contrary to the Basic Principles among the Socialist Countries), *Viaţa Economică*, no. 24 (June 5, 1964), 15–34; George Ciorănescu, "Ein sowjetischer Teilungsplan. Der Widerstand Rumaenien," *Der Europaeische Osten*, no. 118 (January 1965), 23–32.

    13. "Tratat de Prietenie, Colaborare, şi Asistenţă Mutuală intre R.S. România şi R.S. Cehoslovacia" (Friendship, Cooperation and Mutual Assistance Treaty between SR Romania and SR Czech-

oslovakia), *Scînteia*, August 19, 1968; Nicolae Ceauşescu, speech at Bucharest popular meeting and speech before the Great National Assembly, *Scînteia*, August 22, 23, 1968.

14. Anneli Maier, *Romanian Media Comment on Poland*, RFER, *Background Report*, no. 5 (January 15, 1981) (Romania).

15. George Ciorănescu, *Romanian-Soviet Relations at the Start of the New Year*, RFER, *Background Report*, no. 13 (January 19, 1983) (Romania).

16. Enver Hoxha, *Reflections on China* 1 (Tirana: Nentori lishing House, 1979), 513.

17. Jacques Lévesque, *Le Conflit Sino-Soviétique et l'Europe de l'Est. Ses Incidences sur les Conflits Soviéto-Polonais et Soviéto-Roumain* (Montreal: Les Presses de l'Université de Montréal, 1970), 126ff.

18. George Ciorănescu, *Hua Visits Ceauşescu*, RFER, *Background Report*, no. 143 (June 23, 1983) (Eastern Europe); Patrick Moore, *Hua Kuo-feng in Romania*, RFER, *Background Report*, no. 187 (August 24, 1978) (Romania); George Ciorănescu, *Ceauşescu's Asian Trip*, RFER, *Background Report*, no. 259 (December 16, 1982) (Romania).

19. Enver Hoxha, *Reflections*, 589.

20. *Zeri i Populit*, March 24, 1968; Enver Hoxha, *The Hrushchevists*, ATA, October 9, 10, 1980; Zanga, *Albanian Leader's "Reflections on China,"* 2 RFE, (November 23, 1977):F-561–566.

21. Aurel Braun, *Romanian Foreign Policy Since 1965; The Political and Military Limits of Autonomy* (New York: Praeger, 1978), 211; Walter M. Bacon, "Romanian Military Policy in the 1980s," in Stephen Kertesz, *The Fate of East Central Europe and Failures of American Policy* (Notre Dame, Ind.: University of Notre Dame, 1956), 202–218; Robert W. Clawson and Lawrence S. Kaplan, *The Warsaw Pact: Political Purpose and Military Means* (Wilmington, Del.: Scholarly Resources Inc., 1982).

22. Nicolae Ceauşescu, speech at Bucharest popular meeting, *Scînteia*, August 22, 1968.

23. *Scînteia*, November 27, 28, 29, and 30, 1978.

24. *Legea de Organizarea Apărării Naţionale a RSR* (Bill on RSR's National Defense Organization), Buletinul Oficial, no. 160, December 29, 1972.

25. RFER, *Romanian Situation Report*, no. 15, August 30, 1983.

26. *Scînteia*, August 23, 1983; RFER, *Romanian Situation Report*, no. 16, September 16, 1983.

5

The American Connection

Nestor Ratesh

"In terms of geopolitical symmetry, America should be to Romania what Russia is to Cuba." This amazing statement is said to have been made by a Romanian official at a closed RCP meeting in the midst of the euphoria of 1969, the year Richard Nixon made his trip to Romania, the first visit ever by a U.S. president to a East European country. As it turned out, nothing of the sort was being considered in either Bucharest or Washington, although it may have been feared in Moscow. Whereas the Castro regime had long since become a Soviet surrogate, at no point was the Romanian leadership either prepared or able to shelve communism or leave the Soviet bloc. The Romanian independence that took shape after 1964 actually was nothing more than a minor irritation, never a blow the Soviets could not absorb or a challenge they could not meet. Nevertheless, in a certain way, the symmetry is not all nonsense; in an attempt to balance the overwhelming influence of a nearby superpower a small country may move closer to the rival superpower.

The political dimension of the U.S.-Romanian relationship has too often been thought to be one-sided, mostly because Washington has indeed described its links to Romania primarily in political terms, while Romania has emphasized the economic benefits. Still, for the Romanians the U.S. connection has been of great significance in their desire to multiply and diversify their relations with the rest of the world in order to assert their autonomy in the Communist bloc. By developing a strong link with China and the United States, Bucharest was striving to balance its political and economic dependence on the Soviet Union. This link also gave the Romanian leadership an opportunity to play a role in international diplomacy as a means of enhancing the nationalistic pride of its people, expanding its maneuverability on the world scene, and, in the process, satisfying the personal ambitions of an emerging self-centered Romanian leader. Economic benefits were certainly an important consideration for the Romanians in seeking expanded links with the United States, but hardly the main incentive. The principal concern was political in nature, a need to consolidate and perhaps expand their autonomy, and, therefore, a basic national imperative well beyond the benefits of trade.

The U.S.-Romanian relationship had a laborious start, an uneven development, a bad fall, and then a slow rise to the current plateau, which seems safe although it is not a very lofty one. Over the years, Washington showed a shifting interest in the relationship, often corresponding to the changing goals and approaches of U.S. foreign policy. As for the Romanian leadership, it did demonstrate a steady interest in the U.S. connection, but its erratic behavior did a good deal of harm, some of which is possibly permanent.

Washington did not initially respond eagerly to Romania's advances. At the time the Romanian regime turned to a more independent foreign policy in 1964, the Johnson administration had already articulated its "bridge building" policy toward Eastern Europe, but it was never really implemented, partly because of its overwhelming preoccupation with Vietnam. In any case, the United States was not sure of the new Romanian outlook until after the 1968 invasion of Czechoslovakia, which Bucharest refused to join and which it strongly condemned. One year later, and five years after the initial start of Romania's dissent, the new Nixon administration finally did pay attention to Romania – in the dramatic form of a presidential trip to Bucharest. According to Henry Kissinger's memoirs, one factor in this growing interest in Romania was Nixon's sentimental attachment to the country that had grown out of a visit he had made to Bucharest as a private citizen in 1967, during which he was very well received by Romanian leaders.[1] In political terms, however, the White House conceived of the trip as part of an effort to enlist Soviet cooperation to help end the war in Vietnam. Kissinger writes that Nixon's purpose was "to remind Moscow that he had options toward Eastern Europe and also toward the People's Republic of China, of which Romania was a sometime supporter."[2]

For whatever reasons, the concern with Eastern Europe in general and the Romanian connection in particular were clearly subordinated to the central issue of the U.S.-Soviet relationship. This was an idea that at a later date produced the so-called Sonnenfeldt Doctrine, which argued that because Eastern Europe was within the "scope and area of natural interest" of the Soviet Union, any "excessive action" on the part of the United States toward the countries of that area would be counterproductive. It is interesting to note that the Romanians, somewhat amazingly, greatly benefited from such policies, which were otherwise harmful to East European pluralism. This can be explained by Nixon's warm feelings toward Romania and by Bucharest's willingness to play an intermediary role between the United States and China and later in the Middle East.[3]

Nevertheless, Romania was not to receive the top prize, the most favored nation status (MFN), until six years after Nixon's 1969 trip. And even then, this did not come about without intense lobbying in Washington by many Romanian emissaries, including President Ceauşescu himself. For Bucharest it was not simply a question of trade benefits, but also a symbol of political preference, a significant momentum to bilateral exchanges, and a special standing in the Soviet bloc. In fact, the Romanians accepted what the Soviet Union had previously rejected, namely a strictly conditioned preferential treatment under the provisions of the Jackson-

Vanik Amendment that linked MFN status to free emigration. Even though the Romanian government had managed to avoid giving public assurances on its emigration policies, the Romanians admitted to the principle of linkage and offered private assurances at the beginning of the process as well as each year thereafter at the time of renewal of the MFN status.

Romanian statements were not, however, matched by their actual behavior. While emigration to the United States did grow steadily, Jewish emigration to Israel declined.[4] Further, emigration procedures became more cumbersome while harassment of would-be emigrants intensified. That happened at a time when the Carter administration placed human rights at the heart of U.S. foreign policy. This new emphasis clearly worked against the Romanian regime, which was increasingly seen in the West as one of the most repressive in Eastern Europe.

At the same time, a new approach to Eastern Europe was being articulated by the Carter administration, one that had developed gradually since the Nixon years. It was the so-called differentiation policy, according to which Eastern Europe should not be seen as a monolithic bloc but rather as an area populated by countries of great historic, geographic, ethnic, and cultural diversity, a diversity that still existed despite the imposition of an alien ideology. This approach was incorporated in a largely new world perspective, one that deemphasized the U.S.-Soviet relationship by stressing the concept of a triangular world power system that included China and that extended U.S. links to the Third World. Eastern Europe was to be treated not merely as a function of the U.S.-Soviet relationship, but as a separate entity with diverse contours. In this context, Romania's relative independence, which was no longer a striking feature and was even for the Soviets an accepted (and at times perhaps beneficial) fact of life, appeared to be of less consequence. Moreover, the worsening human rights record severely eroded the great political capital Romania had accumulated in Washington. It is interesting to note that, although Ceauşescu was invited to

Washington in 1978, Carter never went to Bucharest in spite of insistent private invitations from the Romanians. Moreover, the U.S. president visited Poland and Yugoslavia and intentionally skipped Romania, to the great dismay of the Romanian regime.[5] Secretary of State Cyrus Vance did schedule a visit to Bucharest in December of 1979, but cancelled it in the aftermath of the Soviet invasion of Afghanistan.

Both the differentiation approach and the human rights policy tilted the Carter administration toward a more favorable recognition of Hungary.[6] At the same time, Americans were also fascinated by the astonishing pace of the Polish liberalization with the emergence of Solidarity, a development that made the Romanian experiment in independence in foreign policy while it continued domestic repression look much less attractive.

The U.S.-Romanian political relationship lost a good deal of interest and priority in Washington even as trade picked up, exceeding the $1 billion mark in 1980. The yearly renewal of MFN in Congress, however, became a more difficult exercise, with stronger criticism being directed not only at Romania's emigration policies but also at its general human rights record. Such issues as religious persecution and ethnic discrimination were raised constantly by different members of Congress and human rights organizations. Spokesmen of neoprotestant groups and the Hungarian community in the United States, in addition to the witnesses interested in the emigration issue, regularly denounced the Romanian government and opposed the renewal of the preferential treatment granted to Romania. At the urging of the Carter administration, however, Romania's MFN was renewed, though with less enthusiasm each year. By the time President Reagan took office, the U.S.-Romanian link had been downgraded to a mere third place in Washington's list of East European priorities.

The Romanian leadership was known to have preferred Reagan over Carter in the 1980 presidential campaign because of an almost mystical belief that, for Bucharest, Republicans were better than Democrats. It hoped, perhaps, for a new Nixon. Romanian leaders apparently calculated that a tougher anti-Soviet stand would tend to imply more recognition for their dissent from Moscow and would therefore shelve, temper, or at least balance out the human rights criticism. In other words, they bet on a restoration of the predominance of geopolitical considerations over human rights issues. They remembered Reagan's sharp attack on the Sonnenfeldt Doctrine in the 1976 primaries, in which Reagan made Eastern Europe a campaign issue.[7]

The Romanian expectations, not entirely unjustified, did not, however, square with the reality of the Reagan administration's policies, at least during the first two years of its first term. Reagan continued the differentiation policy of the Carter administration. If there was a deemphasis on human rights concerns, it did not apply to the situation in Communist nations. If anything, the denunciation of communism in general became a theme of presidential pronouncements, and a doctrinal anticommunism – not just anti-Sovietism – evolved not only as a rhetorical trait but, in certain instances, as a policy component. With the reversal of conditions in Poland, local Communist repression began to be considered almost as much of an evil as direct Soviet domination.

The geopolitical consideration did grow in significance and might have worked in Romania's favor had the Romanian regime done something to improve its image and revive its independence in some perceivable way.[8] But the opposite happened. Two developments surfaced that diminished Romania's reputation even more, in fact, to the lowest point in almost two decades. First, fearing that the impact of the events in Poland would spread to Romania, Ceauşescu's regime moved to suppress all political dissent, expanding its repression across the borders to its opponents abroad. Second, Romania suffered from a severe financial crunch. With a foreign debt of between $10–13 billion, the Romanian government was unable to repay any of the principal owed to Western banks and governments, although it did continue interest payments. It could not obtain any new significant credits in the West, however, except for a multiyear financial loan from the International Monetary Fund. The country was caught in what the *New York Times* called "a disastrous economic plight."[9]

Ceaușescu's reaction was to blame the West for his trouble, something he apparently really believed. This does not make it more credible, but it helps to explain his actions, which, in turn, caused a serious regression in Romania's ties with the United States and the West in general. In August 1982, *New York Times* writer John B. Oakes described the Romanian president as "infuriated" by the virtual cutoff of credit from the West. In an interview with Oakes, Ceaușescu stated his belief that such tough economic measures, particularly on the part of the United States, were politically rather than economically motivated and were both politically and economically counterproductive. In that same interview, he traced Romania's economic difficulties not to his own faulty policies, but, instead, to the United States. "Mr. Ceaușescu believes," Oakes wrote,

> that the United States as a global creditor is attempting to shift the burden of paying for its arms program to the rest of the world through high interest policies designed to help cover the cost of the American arms buildup. Such policies tend to drive East European nations even further away from the West.[10]

Few, if any, observers at the time viewed this statement as a portent of drastic moves that would, at least temporarily, pull Romania away from the West. After all, that same month Romanian diplomats and emissaries were trying hard to preserve its MFN status in the face of the strongest congressional opposition ever. The Romanians were successful in the end by displaying a certain amount of flexibility and offering to improve emigration procedures. In October of 1982, Elliott Abrams, assistant secretary of state for human rights, negotiated a verbal agreement in Bucharest, which was to be put into writing and provide for an end to the harassment of prospective emigrants and some changes in the long and burdensome government emigration procedures. Upon his return from Bucharest, Abrams granted an interview to Radio Free Europe (RFE), in which he described his talks as "constructive" and praised his Romanian counterparts as "cooperative." At the same time, he called the Romanian regime "an extremely oppressive communist dictatorship" with a "deplorable, terrible" human rights record. The interview, broadcast in full by RFE on October 18, 1982, reportedly angered the Romanian president, heightening his misgivings and suspicions about the United States.

A few days later, disregarding assurances previously given to the U.S. government and contrary to the spirit of the agreement just concluded with U.S. officials, Mr. Ceauşescu signed the decree imposing an education tax and several other restrictions on emigration, a move that precipitated a deep crisis in U.S.-Romanian relations.[11]

The new Romanian legislation drastically narrowed Washington's options. Until the decree was signed, the administration and the Congress could decide more or less subjectively whether Romania was complying fully with the requirements of the Trade Act of 1974. Once the decree was operative, however, the issue became quite clear: section 402 of the Trade Act, known as the Jackson-Vanik Amendment, specifically prohibits the granting of MFN status to any non-market country that imposes "more than a nominal charge on any of its citizens who want to emigrate to a country of their choice." With the decree in place, there was no way Romania could keep its MFN status.

President Reagan acted very reluctantly, however. He lost no opportunity to make sure the Romanians understood the risks and consequences of their move and, in fact, waited four months, until the actual implementation of the decree, before announcing a decision to terminate MFN status for Romania.[12] Even then it was not an immediate cutoff, but a projected termination for June 30, 1983, if Romania did not cease applying the education tax by that date. The delay was meant, on the one hand, to enable U.S. companies doing business with Romania to adjust gradually to the new situation and minimize their losses and, on the other hand, to offer the Romanians a last chance for reconsideration.

Reagan's reluctance was not without motivation. This time it was not just another case of erosion in U.S.-Romanian relations; it was a serious, indeed even dramatic setback, which brought the relationship dangerously close to an irreparable rift. Furthermore, it seemed to be part of a reverse in Romania's overall foreign policy, as the new decree affected Romania's strong links with West Germany (the destination of the overwhelming majority of Romanian emigrants) and Israel, as well. It was followed by a chill between Bucharest and Paris after a series of assassination attempts against two prominent opponents of the Romanian regime living in France. Statements issued by the leadership in Bucharest indicated a deep disappointment with its relationship with the West and a trend toward economic isolationism. The German newspaper, *Frankfurter Allgemeine Zeitung*, pointed to "deliberate acts of worsening Romania's relations with the West."[13] The course taken by Ceauşescu raised serious questions as to whether Romania was returning to a closer relationship with the Soviet Union.

Amazingly though, the tensions with the West did not seem to bring about any rapprochement with Moscow at that time. If anything, Romanian-Soviet ideological disputes had multiplied: the quarrels over the CMEA's integration plans had grown more acute; there was the growing assertiveness of Romanian historians about Bessarabia; and Ceauşescu's relationship with Andropov turned out to be more precarious than the one he had had with Brezhnev. In fact, it looked like Bucharest was heading for a simultaneous chill with both the West and the East. Added to the huge economic losses that Romania would have taken just by being denied MFN status in the United States at a time of severe financial strains, this political ineptitude suggested a picture of irrationality and of erratic behavior at the top of the Romanian leadership.[14]

Washington hoped that, given more time, the Romanians would find a face-saving solution and return to a more rational approach. The policy worked. Following extensive bilateral discussions, an understanding was reached between the two governments whereby the Romanians would stop implementing the emigration decree and improve some of its emigration procedures and in return the United States would extend the nondiscriminatory treatment for another year. The deal was sealed in an exchange of letters between Reagan and Ceauşescu, and Congress went along. The rift in U.S.-Romanian relations was avoided.

Having reached rock-bottom in the midst of the crisis, U.S.-Romanian relations returned to an acceptable level. The improvement was speeded by the need of the U.S. administration to assert itself in Eastern Europe in view of existing or anticipated tensions with the Soviet Union. With an election year quickly approaching, a decision was made to give high level attention to Hungary and Romania – the two countries of the area that met Washington's requirement for liberal domestic policies and/or an independent foreign policy before all energies became focused on the campaign. In late September 1983, Vice President Bush went to Bucharest and Budapest for highly visible visits that were supposed to draw a line between the "good" and the "bad" in Eastern Europe. Fearing that the message might be ignored, Mr. Bush gave a speech in Vienna at the end of his trip, making clear that the United States

> will engage in closer political, economic and cultural relations with countries such as Hungary and Romania which assert greater openness or independence. . . . We will not reward closed societies and belligerent policies – countries such as Bulgaria and Czechoslovakia, which continue to flagrantly violate the most fundamental human rights, and countries such as East Germany and, again, Bulgaria which act as proxies to the Soviets. . . . [15]

The vice president's trip to Bucharest was followed by a visit from Secretary of Commerce Malcolm Baldrige in October and a congressional mission in December. Romanian

Foreign Minister Stefan Andrei also came to Washington in October 1983 and again in February of 1984. In late February 1984, a U.S.-Romanian dialogue on human rights took place in Washington at a fairly high level of representation on both sides.

The Romanian leadership seemed delighted by the sudden distinction, coming not long after being denounced by the Reagan administration in words such as "draconic" and "oppressive." Then, a few months later, Romanian participation at the Los Angeles Olympics, in spite of the Soviet-inspired boycott, was very well received in the United States, providing a few moments of short lived euphoria in the relationship.

Still, except for the Olympic episode, 1984 was not a particularly warm or fruitful year for U.S.-Romanian relations. There was a certain amount of visibility in the relationship, but little substance. One important component continues to be a U.S. desire to encourage diversity in the Soviet bloc and Romania's insistence on a measure of autonomy in its foreign policy. Bucharest's occasional resistance to some Soviet initiatives within the Warsaw Pact and the CMEA and its (perhaps overpublicized) differences in international matters are seen by U.S. officials as irksome to Moscow, sometimes creating an excuse or a cover for the assertiveness of other Communist nations. Washington terms this "the nuisance factor."

But, more often than not, Romania's dissent is marginal and its real benefit to the West is elusive. Moreover, certain changes seemed to have occurred in 1984 in Romania's relationship with the Soviet Union that would tend to raise questions about the real extent of the regime's independence. These developments seemed related to the death of Yuri Andropov and Konstantin Chernenko's ascent to the top job in the Kremlin. The strains between the two countries appeared to have eased considerably. All outside signs pointed to a much better personal rapport between Ceauşescu and Chernenko. The Romanian leader's disappointment with the West, the beating he takes in the Western media, his economic and financial troubles, and the uneasiness at home may have contributed to this rapprochement, if this is what it is. In any case, it includes some not-so-subtle changes in Romania's stand on the INF issue to conform more closely with the Soviet position and a greater Romanian willingness to participate in the Warsaw Pact and CMEA dealings. It is too early to know what impact the new transfer of power in the Kremlin will have on Soviet-Romanian relations.

At the same time, in a somewhat new East European context, Romania is hardly the only card – and is perhaps not even the best card – the United States can play in the Soviets' backyard. Poland, for all its problems, is much more diverse, dynamic, and prone to change and is a country in whose fate the United States has much more of an interest and is much better able to influence. Hungary, with a more acceptable domestic policy, has begun to inch away from Soviet tutelage in some areas of foreign policy as well, and East Germany has exhibited a few interesting signs of autonomy.

In addition, there are a few features of Romania's independence that have lost their attraction or usefulness for the United States. Romania's role as an intermediary in diplomatic exchanges, for example, is not in demand anymore. The United States has direct contacts with the Chinese as does Israel with Egypt. U.S. diplomacy is connected either directly or indirectly to virtually every side in the Middle East conflict. It is not only that the Romanians may have lost some of their credibility as intermediaries, but more than that, it is that the world has changed in a way that diminishes Romania's diplomatic role.

Finally, the nature of the Romanian regime makes it an embarrassment for the United States and other Western nations to be associated too closely with Bucharest. Its human rights record is consistently censured in official U.S. statements or presidential reports. Although the emigration issue has been defused somewhat, due to developments largely unrelated to the Romanian government's actual performance[16], religious persecution, ethnic discrimination, and political oppression are more prominent in U.S. criticism. A lingering effect from the emigration crisis was still being felt in early 1985. For one thing, the credibility of the Romanian government remained badly damaged, compounded by a suspicion of foul play. The unreliability of its promises and its propensity for sudden and erratic turns have left a lasting impression in Washington.

The only dynamic area of U.S.-Romanian relations (in relative terms) is trade. As expected, the strong recovery in the United States and a certain improvement in Romania's financial situation have provided an impetus to bilateral trade, even though it stopped short of some of the magnificent (and unrealistic) targets set by the Romanians.[17] In fact, trade recovered to the levels of the early 1980s, but with a sharply different structure. While in 1980 the United States had a $407.7 million trade surplus, it registered a $327 million deficit in 1983. The almost uninterrupted string of U.S. trade surpluses of previous years actually ended in 1981, coinciding with Romania's financial crunch and a major unilateral compression of trade. The U.S. trade deficit with Romania virtually doubled in the following three years and is estimated to have reached well over $400 million in 1984, an almost exact reversal of the U.S.-Romanian trade situation in 1980. This was accomplished by drastic reductions in Romania's purchases of U.S. food and live animals as well as machinery and transportation equipment.[18] In total trade, Romania has become the main partner of the United States in Eastern Europe, with Poland, which had this distinction years ago, second and Hungary a distant third.[19]

Nevertheless, the Romanians continue to press the U.S. administration for measures that would speed up bilateral trade. U.S. officials respond that there is very little they can do, because the U.S. economy is not government controlled. If anything, the United States is likely to try to close the trade gap with Romania, although questions are sometimes raised as to whether it is not in the U.S. interest to enable Romania to repay its debt and help make its independence more attractive economically to the other East European nations. On the other hand, should the United States compensate for the failures of a highly centralized, ineptly managed economy? Vice President Bush gave a straightforward answer in his Vienna speech:

> We cannot be expected to shore up a nation's economy if the Government refuses to institute the most basic economic reform. . . . It is by now abundantly clear that highly centralized, command economies cannot fulfill the basic needs of their populations, let alone remain competitive in world markets or keep pace with technological advancement.[20]

The future of U.S.-Romanian relations is hard to predict. The fact that the relationship between the two countries has depended to such an extent on geopolitical considerations leaves the situation vulnerable to the ups and downs of U.S.-Soviet relations. Unless the United States and Romania find areas of real political convergence, of ample and mutually beneficial economic cooperation, and of productive dialogue on human rights, and unless the Romanian regime gains more respectability and acceptability beyond the status of "necessary in spite of," the relationship may drag on at its present plateau. It has been a peculiar relationship all along. Peculiarity is transient and normality tends to claim its rights sooner or later.

Notes

1. "Nixon never forgot courtesies of this kind. . . . " Henry A. Kissinger, *The White House Years* (Boston, Mass.: Little, Brown & Co., 1979), 156.

2. Ibid., 144–145.

3. Kissinger offers rare insight into this role, particularly with regard to China. According to him, neither China nor the United States totally trusted the Romanian leadership. He describes many instances in which the Chinese preferred to use the Pakistanis as a channel rather than the Romanians. "It would be difficult for Bucharest to avoid briefing Moscow." (Ibid., 704.) Later, Kissinger notes that he and Zhou En-lai had come to the same conclusion

regarding Romania: "It was simply too exposed, too tempted by its own necessities and too unfortunately located geographically to handle the last phase of setting up contacts, however helpful it had been at earlier stages." (Ibid., 714.)

4. According to U.S. State Department data, emigration to the United States has risen more than eightfold since the granting of MFN to Romania. The same data show that emigration to Israel decreased almost threefold, while emigration to West Germany increased more than three times. The following table presents the annual Romanian emigration to the United States, Israel, and West Germany during the period 1973–1983. The figures represent immigrant visas or similar documentation issued by the respective embassies in Bucharest in the calendar year indicated and reported to Congress by the State Department:

Year	United States	Israel	West Germany
1973	469	4,000 (approx.)	*
1974	407	3,700 (approx.)	*

Most Favored Nation Treatment granted in 1975

Year	United States	Israel	West Germany
1975	890	2,000 (approx.)	4,085
1976	1,021	1,989	2,720
1977	1,240	1,334	9,237
1978	1,666	1,140	9,827
1979	1,552	976	7,957
1980	2,886	1,061	12,946
1981	2,352	1,012	8,619
1982	2,381	1,474	11,546
1983	3,499	1,331	13,957

*not available

5. Romanian President Nicolae Ceauşescu visited Washington four times: in 1970, 1973, 1975, and 1978. President Nixon went to Bucharest in 1969 and President Ford in 1975. In his memoirs, former National Security Adviser Zbigniew Brzezinski recalls that, when discussing a planned presidential visit to Poland, he also mentioned to President Carter the possibility of his going to Romania instead. "Carter's reaction was negative," Brzezinski writes. "He pointed out that his two predecessors had gone to Romania

and there was no point in a third visit." Zbigniew Brzezinski, *Power and Principle* (New York: Farrar, Straus & Giroux, 1983), 297.

6. In a highly symbolic act, the United States returned the crown of St. Stephen to Hungary in January 1978. Two months later, Hungary was granted MFN status. One objective cited by Brzezinski was "to encourage the evolution of Hungarian-style communism." (Ibid., 299.)

7. Reagan charged that the Ford administration had advocated that "the captive nations should give up a claim of national sovereignty and simply become part of the Soviet Union." (*New York Times*, April 1976.) Ford termed the charge "ridiculous," repudiating the Sonnenfeldt Doctrine, while the State Department released secret documents on U.S. policy toward Eastern Europe to prove that the doctrine had no bearing on the administration's real approach. (*New York Times*, April 1976.)

8. In fact, in February 1981, the Reagan administration made a major gesture toward Romania by sending Secretary of State Alexander Haig on a trip to Bucharest.

9. *New York Times*, August 5, 1982.

10. *New York Times*, August 6, 1982.

11. The decree was made into law on October 22, 1982, but actual implementation began only in February 1983. Under the decree, all emigrants were to be required to repay, in convertible currency, the costs of their education and training beyond the compulsory level before they could leave.

12. U.S. officials carefully explained the situation to the Romanians in Washington and Bucharest. Soon after the introduction of the "emigration tax," President Reagan sent a message to President Ceauşescu urging that the measure be rescinded to avoid a crisis in relations. Foreign Trade Deputy Minister Paule Prioteasa, while on a visit to Washington in November 1982, was warned that MFN was in serious jeopardy. U.S. Ambassador to Bucharest David Funderburk made the U.S. position clear to different Romanian officials, including President Ceauşescu. In January 1983, Under Secretary of State Lawrence S. Eagleburger was sent to Romania as a special presidential envoy carrying a message from Reagan to Ceauşescu. A few days later, a congressional delegation met in Bucharest with the Romanian president, warning him that chances were very strong that Congress would deny his

country MFN status. President Reagan's statement was issued by the White House on March 4, 1983.

13. *Frankfurter Allgemeine Zeitung*, February 14, 1983.

14. A U.S. Commerce Department analysis found that 75 of Romania's top 80 exports to the United States would have become significantly less competitive without MFN. Twenty-nine of them would have been forced out of the U.S. market by tariff increases in the 30–50 percent range. The department estimated that, during the first year following termination of the MFN status, Romanian exports to the United States would have been about $200 million less than otherwise. The potential commercial loss to Romania from 1984 to 1988 was put up to $2 billion. Moreover, expiration of MFN would have rendered Romania ineligible to receive U.S. government credits and credit guarantees as well.

15. *Washington Post*, September 22, 1983.

16. Two such developments are noticeable. First, a Supreme Court decision, known as the Chadha decision (June 23, 1983), held the so-called "legislative veto" unconstitutional. According to most legal experts, Section 402 of the Trade Act (i.e., the Jackson-Vanik Amendment) is a form of "legislative veto." Although the administration has stated that it was prepared to continue the MFN process, as provided by the amendment, it is uncertain whether the Congress can still terminate MFN with a resolution of disapproval passed by majority vote in either house should it disagree with the presidential waiver. In other words, the Jackson-Vanik Amendment may have lost some of its credibility.

Second, U.S. immigration laws and regulations have limited the number of Romanian immigrants admitted to the United States. With a sizeable backlog of people who have been issued passports by the Romanian government but are unable to leave Romania for lack of U.S. entry visas, the pressure on the Romanian government from Washington on the emigration issue has eased considerably.

17. One target set by the Romanian government, which U.S. experts consider unrealistic, provides for total U.S.-Romanian trade to reach the $2 billion mark by 1985.

18. For a more detailed look at the development of U.S.-Romanian trade in the years 1976 to 1984, the following is a table compiled from official statistics of the U.S. Department of Commerce (in million dollars):

	1976	1977	1978	1979	1980	1981	1982	1983	1984 (first 6 months)
U.S. Exports	249.0	259.0	317.4	500.5	720.2	503.8	223.2	186.1	157.7
U.S. Imports	198.8	233.3	346.6	329.3	312.5	559.4	339.1	513.1	389.2
Total Trade	447.8	492.7	664.0	829.8	1032.7	1063.2	572.3	699.2	546.9

19. For a more detailed comparison, see the following table on U.S. trade with Eastern Europe in the last five years, compiled from official statistics of the U.S. Department of Commerce (total trade in million dollars):

Country	1980	1981	1982	1983	1984 (first six months)
Romania	1,032.4	1,063.2	572.3	699.2	546.9
Poland	1,125.3	1,040.4	505.4	513.0	263.0
Hungary	186.5	205.4	201.0	268.0	133.9
East Germany	520.2	340.2	274.3	197.1	117.3
Czechoslovakia	246.2	149.6	145.1	120.7	59.0
Bulgaria	183.5	283.7	131.5	93.6	35.3

20. *Washington Post*, September 22, 1983.

6

The Nationalities Policy: Theory and Practice

Simona Schwerthoeffer

According to the most recent Romanian census, taken in 1977, ethnic minorities account for 11.86 percent of Romania's population of 21.56 million.[1] Hungarians are the largest ethnic group by a substantial margin (7.9 percent), followed by ethnic Germans (1.6 percent) and Gypsies (1.06 percent). Ukrainians, Serbs, Croats and Slovenes, Jews, Russians, Slovaks, Tartars, Turks, and Bulgarians form numerically insignificant groups.

The proportion of ethnic minorities in Romania's population was substantially reduced by the upheavals of World War II. Territorial losses, including the loss of Bessarabia and Northern Bukovina to the USSR in 1940 and again in 1944, and the loss of Southern Dobruja to Bulgaria in 1944 were one important cause because these were territories with a sizeable non-Romanian population. The dislocation of ethnic groups during the war further reduced the ethnic minorities. Ethnic Germans from Bessarabia, Bukovina, and the Dobruja were resettled in the German Reich, others enlisted in the German army or fled with the retreating German forces at the close of the war, and still others were deported as forced laborers to the USSR at the end of the war. Violent acts against Jews in some Romanian territories (Northern Transylvania, Bessarabia, and Bukovina), which were not at that time under Romanian jurisdiction reduced their population severely.[2]

Consequently, whereas the ethnic minorities in Romania accounted for 28.1 percent of the population during the war, the first postwar census, taken in 1948, showed that this percentage had declined substantially – to 14.3 percent.[3] This figure has continued to decline steadily – from 12.1 percent in 1966 to 11.8 percent in 1977 – primarily because of emigration and assimilation.[4]

The Hungarian minority in Romania, according to official Romanian data, currently consists of about 1.7 million persons.[5] The Hungarians are concentrated in Transylvania, partly in the border region adjacent to Hungary. The Szeklers, a people akin to the Magyars, are in the southeast corner of Transylvania.

The approximately 360 thousand Germans are divided into the Transylvanian Saxons (whose ancestors were made frontier guards by the Hungarian kings beginning in the twelfth century) and the Swabians of the Banat (whose forefathers were brought to Romania as colonists by the Habsburgs in the eighteenth century).

The RCP treated the national minorities generally favorably as it consolidated its power. In accordance with Marxist-Leninist doctrine and in line with the Soviet model, the official ideology was that socialism provides for a positive and just solution to the nationalities question. National tensions and conflicts, which are interpreted as a product of capitalistic development, would disappear once the bourgeois system had been overcome. The introduction of socialism would eliminate all forms of exploitation, including national oppression, and would lead to the establishment of fraternal relations among the working people of all nationalities.[6]

In addition to this doctrinal support, during its first years in power the RCP was still under the influence of a substantial number of ethnic functionaries, mainly Hungarians and Jews.[7]

Romania's first Communist constitution (adopted in 1948) guaranteed equal rights to all nationalities, as well as the free use of their mother tongues in the sphere of education, culture, and administration. The rights of special groups were not specifically designated in the document, however.[8]

The treatment of the ethnic Germans in the early postwar years was an exception to the favorable treatment of minorities. In 1945, they were collectively branded as Nazis and dispossessed of their property. About 75 thousand of them were deported for reconstruction work in the USSR.[9] In 1951, about 30 thousand Swabians from the Banat were deported under inhuman conditions to the inhospitable Baragan region in the lower Danube Plain.[10]

The party's generally liberal approach toward minorities reached a climax in 1952 with the creation of the Magyar Autonomous Region (MAR) in the Szekler lands of eastern Transylvania. This administrative district included the most heavily concentrated group of Hungarians in the country, about one-third of the Hungarian population of Romania. The establishment of the MAR was reportedly the result of Soviet pressures.[11] There are indications that Stalin saw political advantages in keeping a strong Hungarian minority in Romania that he could call upon, if he should ever need them to neutralize their fellow Romanians.[12]

A certain shift in the RCP's nationalities policy took place in the mid-1950s. By the late 1940s party membership showed a definite change in ethnic composition. In the course of the massive influx of new party members between 1945 and 1948, the RCP's ranks were swelled by ethnic Romanians. The party thus lost much of its multinational character. In subsequent years this trend was accentuated. In 1955, 79.2 percent of party members were Romanian; by 1968, they accounted for 88.43 percent of the enrollment.[13]

The party's upper echelons also underwent a process of "Romanization." In the power struggle among rival RCP factions, prominent non-Romanian leaders were purged. In 1952, Ana Pauker and Vasile Luca (the former of Jewish descent, the latter of Hungarian) were removed, and in 1957, Iosif Chisinevski (of Jewish descent) was ousted.

The turning point in the treatment of minorities in general, and of the Hungarian minority in particular, was the Hungarian uprising in 1956. The unrest in neighboring Hungary provided Bucharest with an opportunity to exploit the circumstances for its own benefit. In 1960 the boundaries of the MAR were redrawn in a way that reduced the proportion of Hungarians from 77 percent to 62 percent. At the same time, the region's official name was changed by adding the Romanian word *Mures* to the title, which then became the Mures-Magyar Autonomous Region (MMAR). In 1968, during the course of another countrywide territorial-administrative reorganization, apparently carried out mainly for economic reasons, the MMAR was abolished. By 1965, any reference to Hungarian autonomy had been eliminated from the constitution.

Another significant step in the party's tightening of its nationalities policy was the merger of the Bolyai University, in which Hungarian was spoken, with the Babes University in Cluj, in which Romanian was spoken. The measure was presented as part of an effort to combat manifestations of nationalism and isolationism and to strengthen brotherhood among the youth. The merger was part of a package of measures directed against Hungarian university-level educational facilities, involving the Cluj Agronomical Institute, the Medical Institute at Tirgu Mures, and several Hungarian art institutes.

It should be noted here that one of the major complaints of Romania's ethnic minorities since the 1960s, especially of the Hungarians and Germans, has been the amalgamation of minority schools with Romanian educational institutions. Independent minority schools are slowly being turned into minority-language departments attached to Romanian schools.

A factor that was bound to affect the party's nationalities policy was the change in the RCP's relationship with Moscow that emerged in the mid-1960s, as Bucharest gradually began to emphasize Romanian issues while making increasingly fervent appeals to Romanian nationalistic feelings. But it was two decades before leading representatives of the Hungarian minority protested and before knowledge of such action reached the West. The most outstanding among them were Karoly Kiraly, a former alternate member of the RCP Political Executive Committee and a vice chairman of the Hungarian Nationality Council, and Lajos Takacs, candidate member of the RCP Central Committee and also a vice chairman of the Hungarian Nationality Council. These two prominent Communist officials presented to the state and party leadership memoranda criticizing what they called the vast gap between theory and practice in the treatment of the minorities.[14] The catalogue of complaints listed instances of alleged nonobservance of the minorities' constitutional, linguistic, educational, cultural, and political rights, among them the decline in the number of schools teaching in the Hungarian language; the discouragement of the use of the Hungarian language in public; the removal of bilingual signs and announcements in areas with a heavy Hungarian population; the appointment of Romanian-speaking officials to posts in Hungarian-speaking areas; and restrictions on personal and cultural contacts between Transylvanian Hungarians and Hungary. Takacs, a former rector of the University of Cluj-Napoca, not only drew attention to the steady decrease in the number of Hungarian students admitted to universities but also called for the reestablishment of university-level education in which the Romanian and Hungarian languages would be equally recognized and accepted.

In 1982, *Ellenpontok*, a Hungarian-language *samizdat* publication circulating in Romania, published a petition addressed to the Conference on Security and Cooperation in Europe (CSCE) follow-up conference in Madrid.[15] The petition accused the Romanian government of trying to turn Romania into a state without national minorities by threatening the Hungarian minority with cultural extinction and by forcibly dispersing long-established Hungarian communities through the mass influx of Romanian workers into Transylvania to fill new jobs created by industrialization. The document called for the granting of self-government in those areas where Hungarians are in the majority and for the full participation of Transylvanian Hungarians in the cultural life of the entire Hungarian nation. It also requested an international commission to investigate these complaints.

This dissatisfaction on the part of the Hungarian minority was supported by a number of intellectuals from Hungary. The well-known writer Gyula Illyes broke a taboo when he publicly voiced such sentiments. In a daring two-part article calling attention to the problems of the ethnic Hungarians living outside the country, Illyes described the Hungarian minority as suffering "a fate close to apartheid" and as being exposed to an "attempt to socially downgrade a whole community and to destroy it," which amounted to "ethnocide."[16]

Mihnea Gheorghiu, RCP Central Committee member and chairman of the Romanian Academy of Sciences, refuted Illyes's charges in strong terms, attacking him as a man with "an anti-Romanian obsession," whose "painted lies" were a part of the "hateful nationalist agitation of fascist circles of Magyar emigrants." Gheorghiu also implied that Illyes's articles had been approved by an upper political echelon before publication.[17] The polemics continued with a reply by the vice president of the Hungarian Academy of Sciences, Zgigmond Pal Pach, who stated emphatically that the problems of the Hungarians in Romania "will not cease simply by keeping silent."[18]

As was to be expected, the protest of the Hungarian minority met with a harsh response from the Romanian authorities. In 1982 a number of persons associated with *Ellenpontok* were temporarily arrested and reportedly mistreated by the police. Among them were the poet Geza Szoecs, the philosopher Attila Ara-Kovacs, and the professor Karoly Toth. This crackdown spurred cultural personalities in Hungary to send a letter of protest signed by 70 people to the Hungarian government, asking them to intervene on behalf of the Hungarian intellectuals arrested in Romania.

The Hungarian government had long attempted to avoid publicly expressing official concern about the treatment of ethnic Hungarians in Romania. It preferred to raise the issue during high-level bilateral talks. Crucial to this problem were the Ceauşescu-Kadar meetings of June 15–16, 1977 held in the Transylvanian city of Oradea and in Debrecen, Hungary. The Hungarian side laid stress on improvements in the field of tourism and cultural exchanges, with special regard to the border population. It was agreed that two consulates would be established, one in Cluj-Napoca, the other in Debrecen. The joint communiqué published after the meeting stated that nationality questions were an internal affair, but it also said that ethnic groups can act as a link and bridge between countries.[19] Since then high-level bilateral talks, including visits of Hungarian Socialist Workers' Party (HSWP) Central Committee Secretaries Gyorgy Aczel and Peter Varkonyi to Bucharest in the fall of 1982 and Romanian Foreign Minister Stefan Andrei's visit to Budapest in the spring of 1983, have apparently been conducted in a chilly atmosphere.[20]

Romanian-Hungarian friction over the situation of the Hungarian minority acquired an added dimension because it led to a resurgence of the long-standing Romanian-Hungarian argument over Transylvania. The essence of this controversy, which dates back to the late eighteenth century, is that each side offers its own "historical" justification for its claims to Transylvania. According to Romanian historians, Transylvania is the cradle of the Romanian people, and it has been inhabited continuously since time immemorial by ethnic Romanians and their Daco-Roman ancestors.[21] The Hungarians dismiss the Romanian continuity theory and maintain that when the Hungarians arrived in Transylvania in the tenth century the area was deserted.[22]

The book *Word About Transylvania*, by Romanian writer Ion Lancranjan, published in the spring of 1982, further exacerbated the problem.[23] Lancranjan took up the old Romanian-Hungarian arguments in an emotional and vehement tone, laying the historical blame for the tension in Romanian-Hungarian relations on the Hungarian side, even implying that Hungary was one of the neorevisionist states. Although the book met with a favorable response in Romanian intellectual circles, it was assessed as anti-Hungarian in Hungarian quarters in Romania and Hungary. Lancranjan's zeal was then surpassed by a number of articles in the Romanian press describing in full detail atrocities allegedly perpetrated by followers of Miklos Horthy in the fall of 1940 in Northern Transylvania.[24]

The book was reviewed in an apparently officially sanctioned reply by Gyorgy Szaraz, who wrote a lengthy article in *Valosag* and gave an interview broadcast by Radio Budapest.[25] Szaraz called Lancranjan's text "a strange book," which caused "consternation and concern in Hungary" because it proved the author's commitment to "an ethnocratic state, where power is vested not in the unity of *demos* . . . but rather in the unity of *ethnos*, the 'race of one blood, where the tainted, the alien, is unwelcome.'" Since 1982 leading party circles in Hungary have become increasingly willing to assert themselves more decisively on behalf of their conationals in Transylvania.[26]

An unprecedented move in relations among Warsaw Pact countries was the March 13, 1982 publication in the HSWP daily *Nepzabadzag* of a cartoon and satirical text aimed at President Ceauşescu, ridiculing the personality cult and the campaign for Daco-Roman continuity in Transylvania.[27] This was followed by a starkly authoritative statement by HWSP Politburo member and Central Committee Secretary Gyorgy Aczel, the regime's main spokesman on cultural and ideological matters, who lambasted Romania's nationalities policy: "Unfortunately our old faith, namely that the principles of Lenin's nationality policy would assert themselves automatically, proved to be an illusion. What is more, old nationalist views are being brought back to life and attempts are being made to encroach upon people's rights and achieve forced assimilation."[28] Moreover, the guidelines of the HSWP Central Committee for the thirteenth party congress planned for 1985 approved at a Central Committee meeting on November 15, 1984 contains as a new element references to the rights of Magyar ethnic minorities in neighboring countries.[29] The polemical exchanges between two allegedly fraternal socialist countries normally obligated to maintain bloc unity received great attention in the Western press and elsewhere.

The RCP has always maintained that it has correctly solved the nationalities problem by resolutely applying the principles of scientific socialism and by granting full and equal rights to all of the country's citizens irrespective of nationality. Official pronouncements reiterate that the ethnic minorities, officially called "co-inhabiting nationalities," are proportionately represented in party and state bodies and that educational opportunities and cultural facilities are available in all languages. On the other hand, the RCP's stance is unequivocal: Romania is a unitary national state and the ethnic groups are an integral part.

In spite of the officially waged antiemigration campaign, emigration as a "solution" to the nationalities problem has been applied for many years, especially in the case of the Jews and Germans. Emigration has reduced Romania's postwar Jewish population by 93 percent. During the past 35 years more than 350 thousand Jews reportedly have left Romania. Most of them settled in Israel. A major consequence of this mass exodus has been that, of the approximately 40 thousand remaining Jews, about 65 percent are over the age of 60.[30] About 50 percent of the Jewish population lives in the Bucharest area, but Romania still has approximately 60 Jewish settlements, 120 synagogues, 24 Talmud schools, a Yiddish-language theater, and a biweekly newspaper published in Romanian, Hebrew, and Yiddish.[31] If present trends continue, however, Romania's Jewish community will decline in the foreseeable future to the point where it will no longer be possible to speak about a future for Jewish community life.

As regards the German minority, about 100 thousand left Romania between the end of the war and the late 1970s.[32] A large number left for West Germany after 1967, when Bucharest and Bonn established diplomatic relations. A little-publicized five-year accord, reached in 1978, allowed an annual increment of 11 thousand Germans to be unified with their families in return for West German financial payments to Romania.[33] After the expiration of the 1978 agreement, lengthy Romanian-West German negotiations were necessary because Bucharest had introduced a controversial decree requiring all prospective emigrants to reimburse the state in hard currency for the expense of their education or professional training. An accord reached between Romania and West Germany stipulates that German emigration from Romania can continue at the previous pace. Bonn, in turn, agreed to conditions that helped Romania to reduce the burden of the latter's staggering hard currency debt. West Germany also restored its guarantee for private credits in Romania, which had been discontinued in 1982 for financial reasons; it agreed to sign and support the Western agreement rescheduling Romania's debt for 1982; and the 1973 bilateral economic agreement, which would have expired in 1983, was renewed. According to Western reports, the West German government agreed to pay an additional average amount of about DM 8,000 for each German emigrant.[34]

The RCP's stance on the nationalities question was unequivocally expressed by Secretary General Ceaușescu: "In the foreseeable future there will no longer be nationalities in Romania, but only one socialist nation."[35] The notion of the inevitable disappearance of the nationalities at some future point is in line with Leninist doctrine. Soviet leaders, too, made reference to it in official pronouncements on the role and future prospects of the nationalities. As Soviet Communist Party Secretary General Yuri Andropov stated, "Our final goal is clear. It is in Lenin's words not only the drawing closer of nations, but their merging".[36] Dialectically, however, this trend of thought not only admits that the awareness of belonging to a nationality will continue to exist for a long time, it even infers that nationalities can flourish under socialism.

A characteristic feature of the RCP's theses on the nationality issue is that the equality of the rights of nationalities is based primarily on equality in the material sphere. The regime has made repeated claims that, in line with its concern to ensure the harmonious socioeconomic development of all parts of the country, the Hungarian-inhabited areas — especially the underdeveloped Covasna, Harghita, Satu Mare, and

Salaj counties – have been given special priority. The nationalities often perceive industrialization, however, as a mani-
festation of the regime's policy of assimilation. Industrialization is bound to affect the ethnic position of the minorities
adversely, particularly the Hungarians. Many Romanians are
transferred to predominantly Hungarian regions while many
Hungarians have to leave their traditional areas of settle-
ment. Such large scale dispersion, which may be only indirectly linked with a deliberate effort to reduce Hungarian
representation on the part of the regime, can hardly fail to
have a leveling effect on the ethnic groups.

It has been suggested that Moscow is exploiting the
grievances of Romania's minorities for its own ends, applying the traditional principle of divide and rule to play off
Bucharest and Budapest against each other. As the USSR
has its own pronounced nationality problems, however, it can
hardly be assumed that Moscow would want to go too far
in promoting anything that even looks like the revival of nationalistic rivalries.

The problem of Romania's minorities was drawn to the
attention of Western political circles in the period ushered
in by the Helsinki process and by the campaign on behalf of
human rights initiated in the West and echoed by dissidents
in the Communist countries. The status of Romania's national minorities should be discussed within the framework
of the regime's overall poor human rights record and its failure to implement rights subscribed to on paper. In this context, one should refer to remarks made by University of London Professor George Schoepflin, who noted that

> the assessment of the position of a minority under com-
> munist rule is complicated by the problem of gauging
> the extent to which repression is directed particularly
> and with special force at the minority group, as distinct
> from repression that falls on all sections of the popula-
> tion, including minorities, with more or less equal force.[37]

Constitutional rights have very little substance, especially under the dictatorship of the Ceauşescu family. Institu-

tions and organizations have been reduced to window-dressing roles, and the firm grip of the governmental apparatus leaves no room for group autonomy of any kind. Although the strident overtones of the regime's propaganda regarding nationalist issues is undoubtedly liable to irritate minorities and increase resentment on the part of those nationalities, the systematic violation of human rights and the constant decrease in the standard of living weighs heavily on the majority and minorities alike.

Notes

1. *Scînteia*, January 5, 1977.

2. For exact data see Elemer Illyes, *Nationale Minderheiten in Rumaenien. Siebenbuergen im Wandel* (Vienna, 1981), 26–31.

3. *Recensamintul general al populaţiei României din 29 decembrie 1930* II (The General Census of Romania's Population of December 29, 1930); A. Golopenţia and D. C. Georgescu, *Populaţia Republicii Populare Române la 25 ianuarie 1948. Rezultatele provizorii ale recensamantului*, in *Probleme Economice* II (1948) (The Population of the Romanian People's Republic on 25 January 1948. The Provisional Results of the Census).

4. *Republica Socialistă România. Recensamintul populatiei şi locuinţelor din martie 1966* I, Partea I (Bucharest: Direcţia Centrală de Statistică, 1969) (The Socialist Republic of Romania. The Census of Population and Dwellings of March 1966).

5. Estimates in Hungary are that 2.0 million seems to be a more accurate figure. David Zoltan, "Magyars Along Our Borders," *Mozgo Vilag* (July 1982), 38–50.

6. E. Robotos and P. Pruneanu, "Aplicarea invăţăturii marxist-leniniste in problema naţională," *in Zece ani de la Conferinţa Nationala a PCR 1945–1955* ("The Application of Marxist-Leninist Theory to the National Problem" in *Ten Years since the National Conference of the RCP 1945–1955*) (Bucharest: Editura de Stat pentru literatură politică, 1956), 224–252.

7. Throughout the interwar period the CPR had a membership that totaled at no time more than 1,000 and was composed largely of non-Romanian ethnic elements. At that time the party followed Comintern directives, in conflict with Romanian national interests. It propagated the principle of the right of the nationalities

to self-determination, including the right of secession, in the territories newly acquired by Romania after World War I. (See also Robert King, *A History of the Romanian Communist Party* (Stanford, Calif.: Hoover Institution Press, 1980), 27–38.

8. The Paris Peace Treaty concluded with the allies in 1947 provided equal rights for all Romanian citizens. Moreover, when Northern Transylvania (which had been taken from Romania in 1940 under the terms of the Second Vienna Award) was restored to Romania by the Soviet military authorities in March 1945, shortly after the installment of the Soviet-backed government of Dr. Petru Groza, Stalin insisted that "the rights of the nationalities be respected" (c.f. letter from Stalin to Vasile Luca, cited in "The Vienna Verdict and the Solution of the Problem of the Nationalities," *Romanian Review*, 1, no. 2 (June 1946).

9. *Dokumentation der Vertreibung der Deutschen aus Ost-Mitteleuropa* III (Berlin: Bundesministerium fuer Vertriebene, Fluechtlinge und Kriegsgeschaedigte, 1957), 79E. Romania did not expel its Germans however.

10. RCP Secretary General Nicolae Ceaușescu has admitted that "a number of measures which have unjustly affected many people belonging to the German nationality" were taken in the early postwar period ("Expunerea tovarașului Nicolae Ceaușescu la Plenara Consiliului Oamenilor Muncii de Nationalitate Germana") (The Speech of Comrade Nicolae Ceaușescu at the Plenary Session of the Council of the Working People of German Nationality) *România Liberă*, February 21, 1971.

11. Robert King, *Minorities Under Communism*, (Cambridge, Mass.: Harvard University Press, 1973), 149f.

12. Andrew Lundanyi, *Hungarians in Romania and Yugoslavia: A Comparative Study of Communist Nationality Policies* (Baton Rouge, La.: Louisiana State University, 1971), 358.

13. Ibid., 144.

14. Extensive excerpts from Kiraly's memorandum were published by *New York Times*, February 1, 1978. For Takacs' memorandum see *Financial Times* (London), April 25, 1978.

15. *Ellenpontok*, October 8, 1982.

16. *Magyar Nemzet*, December 25, 1977 and January 2, 1978.

17. *Luceafarul*, May 1, 1978.

18. *Elet es Irodalom*, July 8, 1978.

19. RFER, *Romanian Situation Report*, no. 20, (June 22, 1977).

20. Patrick Moore, "Romanian Foreign Minister in Hungary," RFER, *Background Report*, no. 46 (March 7, 1983) (Romania).

21. See also George Cioranescu with Patrick Moore, "Transylvanian Continuity: Romanian Contributions," RFER, *Background Report*, no. 252 (November 21, 1979) (Romania). An authoritative synthesis of the Romanian viewpoint appears in *Transylvania, Ancient Romanian Home,* by Nicolae Ceauşescu's brother, Major General Ilie Ceauşescu. It was issued in 1983 by the Military Publishing House in Bucharest.

22. Differences also became manifest at the fifteenth International Historians' Congress, which was held in Bucharest in October 1980.

23. Ion Lăncrănjan, *Cuvînt despre Transilvania* (Word about Transylvania) (Bucharest: Sport-Turism Publishing House, 1982). See also George Ciorănescu, "An Escalation of Polemics on Transylvania," RFER *Background Report,* no. 162 (August 11, 1982) (Romania).

24. *Anale de Istorie,* no. 3, (1982); "Noaptea Sfintului Bartolomeu" (The Night of St. Bartholomew) *Contemporanul,* April 28, 1978.

25. See also Alfred Reisch and Judith Pataki, "Hungarian-Romanian Polemics over Transylvania Continue," RFER *Background Report,* no. 238 (November 15, 1982) (Hungary).

26. Patrick Moore, "Hungarian-Romanian Currents 1982," RFER (December 4, 1982).

27. RFER, *Hungarian Situation Report* (May 12, 1982).

28. *Nepszabadsag,* January 15, 1983. See also RFER, *Hungarian Situation Report* (January 24, 1983).

29. See Alfred Reisch, RFER, December 6, 1984.

30. Figures cited by Romania's Chief Rabbi Moses Rosen, *New York Times,* August 9, 1982.

31. UPI from Bucharest, January 20, 1978.

32. *Sueddeutsche Zeitung,* January 1980.

33. West German officials avoid confirming reports about lump payments by Bonn to Romania. According to Western reports, the sums paid by Bonn for each German resettler amounted under the terms of the 1978 understanding to an average of about DM 5,000 (RFE correspondent in Bonn, June 1, 1983).

34. Ibid.

35. At the eleventh congress of the RCP, 1974.

36. Radio Moscow, December 21, 1982.

37. George A. Schoepflin, "National Minorities under Communism," in *Eastern Europe in Transition* (Baltimore, Md.: Johns Hopkins University Press, 1966).